A Guide to Managing Earthlings

Earthlings

Charles Herrick

A real person, not a professor

Published by Human Fabric Publishing

Seattle, Washington

A Guide to Managing Earthlings

Printed in the United States of America

Other Books by Charles Herrick

Breath of Kenya, Medicine, Mystery and Women in Rural Kenya

Living alone in a primitive village in Africa, a change of circumstances leads to a new, somewhat dangerous role, in which Charles has to play village doctor treating life-threatening diseases that most of us in the West have never seen. Lots of interesting insights on African life, told with humor, mixed with drama. A greatly expanded version of the original book *Breath of Kenya*, this puts more focus on the eerie rituals and taboos – especially those involving women. More little stories and some added drama.

Purple Boy (Non-fiction, autobiography)

A fascinating, often light-hearted look at a pretty tough childhood, set against the backdrop of a special year running track. This in turn is woven into a psychological exploration of a sleep disorder developed in adulthood. Humor and drama bring forth the message that the human spirit can always triumph.

A Checkerboard (Fiction based on a real story)

A very white enlisted man rides through Mississippi on a bus of only black soldiers. It's the end of World War II and Simpson will prove the power of naiveté in changing the world around him. He settles in northern Mississippi where he courts a Southern Belle, partners with a black house painter and is taken under the wing of an aging matriarch. His cultural tutors are everywhere but led most prominently by an old black butler and a tough army Sergeant who support him through the cultural maze and intrigue of Southern living.

Women in My Office (Self-help and business)

Over the course of several years, the author had the privilege of being a sounding board and sotto voce advisor to women who often had no one else to talk to – including their own husbands. Whether seeking to unlock the career secrets of the male-oriented business world or dealing with infidelity, mood issues, or problems on the home front, they always got sincere counsel. Their stories are told here to help women with the many issues they face, often alone. The book has a mixture of drama and humor; kind of like life itself.

Visit CharlesHerrick.com

Dedicated to all the people who show up every day

to work with their fellow Earthlings,

expecting a fair shake,

decent treatment, and a

bit of recognition for their hard work;

and

to those managers

who honor these most basic expectations.

Somebody has to do something,

and it's just incredibly pathetic

that it has to be us.

Jerry Garcia
The Grateful Dead

TABLE OF CONTENTS

TABLE OF CONTENTS

Disclaimer on IBM Stuff

Part of what you read in the following pages will be based on some of the management training and the varied experiences I enjoyed while working at IBM. It is not in any way to be taken as a statement or restatement of official IBM policy, but rather my view and recollection of how things worked when I was there.

PREFACE
Management Training by Immersion

Barely out of college and not yet shaving every day, I sat in the antique-filled office of one of the wealthiest men in Seattle. I was an IBM trainee working for the division that sold the monster, room-sized mainframe computers. I was supposed to be at lunch listening to IBM Systems Engineers talk shop. My boss was trying to make up for the fact that I was a rare hire with no business or computer science background. I was pre-med, and frankly, after a couple of those lunches he had insisted I attend, I was fully planning to quit and go to medical school.

To save my sanity, I started calling up rich people and asking if I could come and visit them. I phoned Ned Skinner, the owner of the Seahawks. Then I called the president of one of the biggest banks in town. This was kind of fun. So I called a bunch of other people I thought could give me insights on life. They always agreed to meet.

As I sat there that day, surrounded by 18th century furniture and Chinese urns from a couple millennia BC, I got a piece of advice that has stuck with me.

After I told him I had been talking to many successful people, he said to me in a fatherly way, "Charles, please be careful when people tell you how they got to be wealthy. I've just told you about a few bumps and bruises I got when I was your age. But I'll bet some of the people you've been chatting with have gone from point A to the Promised Land without a hiccup. Everything they set out to do, they accomplished. They never missed. Every girl they ever asked out for a date said yes right on the spot – and she was gorgeous, the belle of the ball.

"Guys like that will make you feel like you're getting behind and you'll just never be that good. But the truth is, unless you inherit money – and lots of it – life's hard. And you don't need to be 'that good.' We all screw up, get fired, say stupid things and lose friends. We all get told no, no way, no way in hell, over and over and over again.

"So, know what you want to do, hang in there, and treat people well. You'll get there. And then don't go telling some other guy that comes along later how you had it all figured out and how you never had to break a sweat."

He was right about getting there. And I won't do that to you. The approach here is to have you wander around with me through various situations and discussions. You'll get to look at management as it actually happened – or ought to have happened.

I suppose I could have done this academically. I could have broken things down into logical charts and then tossed in a couple of catchphrases. But I would rather you pick this up by osmosis, learn from my successes, my mistakes, and a few of my odd experiences and then go do the hard job of adapting some pretty good ideas to your own style.

Most managers simply don't have a framework to guide their approach to running a business. The management books that come out now and then are kind of junky. They take one concept and use it as a blunt instrument to whack at everything. I wish it were that simple. Instead, I'll just try to give you the templates I've used and you see if you can apply them. You'll strike out a few times. But this is America; we get about a million times at-bat. So keep swinging.

Management is complex because you're dealing with people. It's best to have a good way of looking at the profession, try your hardest, and get a big kick out of seeing what your employees can do.

Earthlings are amazingly productive when they have decent leadership along with some room to experiment, create, and screw up now and then.

Chapter Zero
The Humane Treatment of Earthlings

If you think about it, acting humanely means not behaving in the way a human would often respond in a particular situation.

Frequently, when I teach a class on management, I get fired in role-play situations where I am playing the part of a "bad" employee. In one particular case, which you'll read about later in the book, I probably deserve to be fired by most companies' standards. I make it easier by being in-your-face obnoxious along with some other serious character flaws. We all feel kinda bad about squashing a harmless crane fly. You could have just cupped it in your hands and tossed it out the door. But when we smash a whining, blood-sucking mosquito, we celebrate. And in the office when we give a jerk what he deserves, it feels a lot better than when we really work over a harmless introvert that just can't seem to do the job very well.

But the "bad" employee gives us the opportunity to show our humanity – to him and to everyone else. We can show grace (the giving of something good that is undeserved) and mercy (the withholding of punishment that is deserved). These are godly characteristics, not naturally felt by us humans and certainly easily overcome by expediency when we get into positions of power.

We as executives and managers can change the world. If we don't do it, somebody else will. And that might not be good. There are two great equalizing forces: social imperative and government. This book is not about sociology or governmental politics. It's about business management. But an underlying theme is the issue of humane treatment of our fellow citizens. It's about down-to-earth, practical management. If you are not a good manager, your people will suffer either directly as a result of your ineptness or as a result of the behaviors you adopt as a coercive taskmaster who cannot lead out of respect but must instead employ manipulation, threats, or perpetual maneuvers to be likable and popular. This book will teach you to manage out of competence which is at its most fundamental level solving the right problems the right way. First what and then how.

If you are a competent manager, you possess one of the two characteristics required for humane management. The other is caring. You simply must care. I was an executive who honestly cared, yet I hurt more people than I should have because I didn't adopt caring as an overarching principle that governed my every decision. It was a casual byproduct of my upbringing and experiences in life. I should have cared for the sake of caring.

Instead, I fired people I should have fired but could have found an alternative to doing so. I pounded on people who were more or less helpless to fight back, just like a tyrant. I withheld opportunities and beneficial treatment from people whom I didn't like – though often for good reason. And in so doing, I spread a wave of hurt to their families and to other humans who came into contact with them. Yet I was viewed as a great guy, by most people.

I remember firing a middle-aged man and sending him home in the middle of the afternoon to tell his wife they no longer had an income. I felt lousy. I wondered how long this lousy feeling would last. I fired him essentially to solve a business problem – my problem. And then I created a personal problem – my problem. But what about that guy and his wife? How did he respond when his wife looked at him and said, "What are we going to do?" My feelings were focused on me, once I had made the decision. Instead, they should have been focused on him (and her!) before I made that decision. In looking back, I could have come up with an alternative but I didn't. I didn't have to. I had the power with very few constraints.

It is time we constrained ourselves, unnaturally. Granted, a business is not legally a democracy. We businesspeople, especially we alpha males, look down on egalitarianism and meekness. But to some extent they need to be practiced by us. We need to get out in front of this trend in society. It's not going away. That's the practicality of it. And a better system of sharing while exercising meekness needs to be practiced by us because it's right. That's the humanity of it.

We leaders need to view ourselves as the head of a tribe because our employees view themselves as members of a tribe, instinctively. They don't want to see themselves as replaceable parts in some organic machine. When we treat them that way, we hurt not only them but everyone around them because we disrupt an instinctive, tribal sense of what should be. Any short-term gain achieved by removing that one part is greatly outweighed by the systemic damage done by creating an environment that is not secure for all. That's the practicality *and* the humanity of it.

Still, doing something inhumane often seems to have immediate advantages; even though when everyone does so, it produces the kind of awful morale and high (70% according to Gallup) degree of employee disenfranchisement that exists in today's work environment. It's a case of the fire in the theater. Here's how that works:

You're sitting in a crowded theater when a fire breaks out. You have a choice: do you walk to the exit in a calm and orderly fashion or do you run for the exit? Unfortunately, it turns out that everyone else has that same choice. So, it comes down to you individually versus them collectively. There are four possible decision alternatives for the theater group, you included. If you walk and they walk, you have a reasonable but not certain chance that you will live. If you run and they run, you all will smash into a big bunch at the exit and you will likely not survive. And if they all run and you just walk, you as an individual will almost certainly die. There is one other possible alternative. If everyone else will calmly walk toward the exit and you run as fast as you can, arms flailing, knocking old ladies aside, you will almost certainly survive. This is *your* best alternative.

This is not unlike what we are faced with in society and, closer to where I'm taking this conversation, in the workplace. If everyone else will just act like it's one big tribe, maybe you as an individual can fire people left and right and pound on "bad" employees and get away with it. You run while all the other manager's stifle their instincts and walk.

But I'm telling you, it doesn't work that way. In the theater emergency, we aren't worried about morale and people's long-term willingness to continue to attend the theater. In the workplace, we should be worried about that but for the last twenty years, we seem to have stopped worrying. We don't train our managers to overcome their base instincts. In fact, we don't train them at all. So they are base and marginally competent when it comes to managing our most precious resource, our fellow human beings. If you don't have a sense of humanity, at least have an awareness of ROI and invest in that very expensive line item – your management team.

It's amazing what you must do to your operating procedures, your management policies, and your day-to-day communications when you commit to a policy to "First, do no harm," as Hippocrates instructed doctors so long ago. In addition to not being able to fire people except in rare instances, you can't lay off workers except for survival reasons, and you must create an environment where people want to show up every day and further the tribe's purpose, thus ensuring the likelihood of both thriving and surviving.

So now what are you going to do? Maybe you need to recognize that there will be lean times and get your people's skills up to where they need to be, including your managers. Perhaps you will also recognize that a whole bunch of your employees are less than perfect and you need to have both a plan for that fact as well as an attitude that will make the best of it. You will have to make that not-so-fine distinction between what you are allowed to do and what you should do. Sure, you can berate an employee in front of others and get away with it. But you should bite your tongue, decide if this situation even warrants a discussion, and then have a professional conversation, one on one, behind closed doors. This book will show you how. It turns out that the best way to have good personal relationships with your employees is to de-personalize the management process and make discussions about performance both objective and collegial.

You can also be a moody SOB and your employees will just have to put up with it and try to time your mood swings. Or you can recognize that such behavior is both hurtful to people and harmful to business and keep your mood swung over to only one side of the positive-negative meter. You can guess which one. At IBM we didn't have to guess. It was in each manager's performance plan: *"You will be upbeat at all times."* Moody managers didn't stay in management long. Your bad moods have a ripple effect that extends all the way to your people's spouses and kids. IBM wanted your mood positive because it's good business. I'm saying do it because it's what humans are supposed to do when they honestly care.

This book can go a long way toward teaching the art of professional management and help make you a better leader. But at best it can only make a plea for you to care about your people, including the offensive ones and the ones that "deserve to be culled" from the tribe.

I once personally witnessed a woman being kicked out of a tribe in rural Africa. It was gruesome. She had no place to go. A big, strong woman, she wept uncontrollably and sobbed in huge spasms as she was pushed along and jeered at by the crowd. I can't go back and fix that and neither can anyone else. I can't go back to that woman who asked her husband, "What are we going to do?" – that husband I sent home without an income one afternoon. But you and I can go back to our tribes with a renewed sense of humanity and an overarching belief that we must care even if we feel just the opposite. That's what professionals do and that's what the most humane earthlings do because caring is ultimately an act, not a feeling. We all have had people who cared for us when they probably didn't particularly *feel* like it. We should pay that forward without trying to keep score. Our parents, our teachers, our coaches, and often our neighbors and friends have fulfilled their roles unilaterally, thank God. We will likely never be in a position to repay them. Now, as we assume this most intimate and impactful role as managers, we can in effect honor their decency by simply treating others the way we would want to be treated.

I actually wrote this chapter last. And while I'm neither a softy nor a bleeding heart, I have learned after a few decades of leading earthlings, that true caring will greatly amplify all the hard-hitting management practices that follow. Don't just feel it. Commit to it and do it. Your business will flourish and your employees will thrive.

6

Chapter One
"WHAT" Trumps "HOW"

Think about all the executives and managers you've watched in action. Most have their strengths and their moments of greatness but most people really are lousy managers. The few naturally good managers probably couldn't tell you why they're good and you probably can't put your finger on it either.

Technically, most people are pretty good at what they do. They know HOW to do stuff. Yet the area of management is treated more as an art or an innate quality. There's a lot more *je ne sais quoi*, than *quoi*. Managers are usually measured by other lousy managers on two things as it relates to management: 1) business results (did they make the sales numbers) and 2) how acidic the hatred level is for the manager. Item 1 almost always trumps item 2 in today's world, where management development is emphasized almost not at all. Where it is emphasized it is mostly for team building among managers or for lawsuit prevention. You probably aren't going to get great leadership out of any of that.

So the problem is that most people know HOW to do things and they come up short on WHAT to do. Therefore, managers spend almost all of their time on the HOW and in so doing, they drive everyone nuts.

Here's the first of many rules you'll see in this book:
People in positions of personnel authority need to focus first, foremost, and almost exclusively, on WHAT, not HOW.

Doing a great job at the wrong WHAT represents a significant portion of much business activity. You simply can't achieve excellence, if even your bad agenda (your What-list) is being executed by a flock of geniuses. (Or is it genii? If you don't know; ask a smart person. Better yet, stand in a crowd of really smart people and say, "Hey, genii." Then see if more than one respond.)

WHAT vs. How actually applies to almost any pursuit. Here's a quote from a book on the art of writing, written 50 years ago. It's clear to everyone that they pre-stole my concept but it's too late to sue them now.

> *"Write with nouns and verbs, not with adjectives and adverbs. The adjective hasn't been built that can pull a weak or inaccurate noun out of a tight place."*

> – William Strunk and E.B. White, *The Elements of Style*, 1959

But back to the comparatively prosaic world of business…

Dealing in WHAT from the top down causes everyone to focus on the same thing but allows them to do it according to their own strengths and in their own manner ... provided the guy at the top knows WHAT to do. That hasn't always worked. Let's look at a recent time in history where it failed altogether.

THE DOTCOM BUST: A CASCADE OF WHAT INTO THE MORASS OF HOW

Early in the year 2000, I was starting to get a funny feeling about the whole dotcom miracle. CEOs of various Internet companies were calling me and asking for a meeting to talk about the "future" of their enterprises.

One such meeting involved a person who had received quite a bit of funding and had burned through millions, while only getting his software-based product to about 15% completion. My company was doing great so he thought it might be a good idea to sweep his completely unrelated business under our umbrella. But after twenty minutes of conversation with him, I still had no idea what his product would actually do when it was completed. I didn't know what business he was in. A few months later, he pulled the plug and investors lost tens of millions of dollars. I might have sunk with him had I joined forces.

These conversations made me think about some of the companies I was providing IT consulting services to. Who were my clients and WHAT did they do or make?

I called the Hardware.com account team in for a quick review. They were getting behind on their AR measurements. As they started to leave the meeting, I asked, "Oh, by the way, what does Hardware.com do?" They explained it to me.

I listened for a bit and then just to make sure I understood I tried an example: "So, if I want a pickax, I just log onto Hardware.com and order one and they'll ship it right to my house?"

"That's right!" came the cheerful response from the account team.

"So," I continued, "Instead of going down the street to Home Depot or Lowe's when I want to dig a hole, I just order my pickax online and wait until it gets mailed to me?"

"Yes, Charles. That's right."

"Get everybody out of that account! Now!" I said, sweating.

"But they're on contract!"

"Get 'em out. As soon as they are at a point where it is fair to the client to break free, get them out."

There was a mad scramble and we got most of the people out, but not before Hardware.com stopped paying its bills. We collected all but about $54,000. We then received a letter in the mail from the company that bought Hardware.com and several other companies. The letter offered me 33 cents on the dollar. I took it without hesitation. Others didn't. They still go to the mailbox every day for their check... and their pickax, I suppose.

In the meantime, I began drying up assignments with other companies. Here's how my side of those conversations went with my employees who sold services to many of the dotcom accounts:

"And what do they do? I see. And how do they make money? I see – selling banner ads. And how long before they... Never mind, get everybody out!"

My belief that all was not right in the technology world was further supported by the number of executives who came to "chat" with me about the status of their company.

Most of the CEOs coming to visit, found me by referral. It was flattering, in a way. One gentleman was about 10 years my senior and his opening remark was, "Charles, a mutual friend suggested I come talk to you. He said you would know WHAT to do."

That was one of the biggest problems of the dotcom era, in addition to unbridled ebullience and greed. The people running those firms were often really smart people who knew how to build really swell technology. And as long as there was lots of money, they appeared to manage just fine. But when things got tight or when clients didn't sign up in droves for their spiffy Internet service, they simply did not know WHAT to do. Then, in addition to showing the world what lousy

CEOs they were, they showed their employees what truly awful managers they were.

The dotcom bust was far more severe and brutal than it had to be. Having a bunch of guys fly airplanes into the World Trade Center didn't help any; but the dotcom companies were already on their way to a nasty denouement due to lack of real leadership.

It turns out that being a CEO is more than an IQ test or a popularity contest. You actually have to know WHAT you're doing.

FORMER DULL ATTEMPTS TO GET THERE FROM HERE

The concept of Management by Objective (MBO) was considered a breakthrough in the effective approach to "managing" the business. It had only one shortcoming; it did not delimit the term "objective." It always started out with some goal, usually a number to be achieved by a given time. And then it quickly morphed into behavioral objectives.

Does anyone remember those horrifyingly trite corporate mission statements that covered everything from image in the marketplace ten years from now to diversity of the workforce and always ended in the phrase *"and have fun!"*? What should have been a sentence or two, turned out to be a paragraph or two of pap that, with a change of a word or two, could have been used by Exxon, an ice cream parlor or a gambling casino. The objective was to show there probably was a purpose for the company's existence - while leaving nothing out of the "statement" and offending no one.

Completely uninspired, you would read the mission statement posted in the copier room and then get called into your manager's office for the following conversation:

Boss:	Fred, you're a good salesman but I'm concerned about what I'm seeing.
Fred:	I'm not sure what you mean.
Boss:	Well, let's start with how much time you've been spending on the phone.
Fred:	I'm a salesman. I prospect. I live in Seattle and my territory is Nebraska. I like to call and set up appointments before I fly to Omaha and knock on doors.
Boss:	You see, that's the problem. You think calling is picking up the phone and I think calling is showing up and selling something. Remember, calls-plus-demonstrations-equals-sales. Are you using the lead form I gave you? It's overdue.
Fred:	No, I use the company CRM system on my laptop. You can look at the summary that is current to the minute. It's online. I've shown it to you twice.
Boss:	*(Long exhale. Looks out window, shakes his head)* What am I going to do with you?

Do you see the objective? The boss's objective is to make Fred a "better" salesman. The objective should be to increase sales and, just as important, to increase market share, client base, client penetration and customer satisfaction. The boss should figure out what it's going to take to get there. Maybe leaving Fred alone and working on other problems is part of that strategy. However, pounding on the employee is a lot easier. Also, when the department makes its numbers, the boss can take full credit, not only for what he did but also for "HOW" Fred did.

You have in the above conversation a boss committing three cardinal sins:

- He labeled his employee. He called Fred "a good salesman." It sounds nice but what happens when Fred's numbers drop? Will he then suddenly become a bad salesman? He's either performing well or he needs to improve. Don't label. Dealing in issues and not personalities will be an important objective of this book. (Calling someone a good salesman is probably not that big a deal. I'm mostly using it to illustrate a point).

- He dealt almost entirely in *how* and not at all in *what*. This will be the underlying theme of this book. One legitimate "how" question is this: "How" does the company prevent its managers from focusing on "how" instead of "what"?

- At the end, he placed the burden to correct the situation on his own shoulders: "What am I going to do with you?" This will be a key shift in philosophy for most managers. The question is this: Should a manager solve problems or should a manager create problems?

I have personally observed leadership in the Third World – primarily Africa and the slums of India. It's all about power. And power is all about telling people how to act. The difference between the Third World and the industrialized world is primarily due to one thing: diffusion of power. People here actually have rights and can therefore plan their lives to some degree. In the Third World, power is owned entirely by one person in any given organization or entity. Success is therefore limited to the competence of the leader who must constantly and often arbitrarily demonstrate his power. He "loans" power to his inner circle, members of which in turn "loan" power to the next layer. Each layer is sycophantic to the layer above it and tyrannical to the layer below.

Despite our sense of egalitarianism, most Western companies are a lot closer to the Third World approach than they should be. We have gone through kind of an arc since the 50's. Back then bosses exercised considerable power and the reason was often "because I said so, that's why!" But then peace, love, beads, bells and incense came along and everybody was starting to get equal – perhaps too equal. But there are still a number of companies who are trending back toward the boss is the boss is the boss. It doesn't work anymore but still, something happens to people when they get into power – just like it does to promising leaders in the Third World when they step in after the evil dictator that had terrorized the country finally gets pushed out. When someone is an underling they vow never to be that awful. Four legs good; two legs bad. But when they're handed the scepter it's four legs good; two legs better. (Orwell *Animal Farm*)

Here is a conversation I witnessed within a company where I was providing consulting services. It was run by Middle Easterners doing about $100 million dollars in PCs and related gear. It was very profitable due to massive control of costs.

Mahmoud is the employee. Hamid is the president.

Mahmoud: Sir, we have five employees starting next week. I need you to sign this requisition for five telephones.

(He hands the requisition slip to Hamid who reads it carefully and then looks up over his glasses at Mahmoud who begins to fidget. Returning to reading the slip, Hamid crosses off something, makes another quick mark, and hands it back to Mahmoud.)

Hamid: You may order four phones.

Mahmoud: Four!? But there are five employees! What   will they do?

Hamid: You may order four.

Mahmoud: But....

(Hamid waves him off and Mahmoud leaves, distraught).

Three weeks later, Hamid summoned Mahmoud to his office.

Hamid: You may now order the fifth phone.

Mahmoud: Thank you, sir. Thank you very much.

(Hamid waves him off. Mahmoud backs out of the room with several little bobbing bows).

Arbitrary decisions demonstrate that your power is above even the laws of reason. This keeps a huge distance between the boss and the employee in terms of hierarchy. This is one of the most salient aspects of power mongering. A potentate governing in the Third World does not care that his country is one giant slum. What he cares about is that he is the undisputed leader.

Oliver Wendell Holmes, the great Supreme Court justice in the 30's said:

"The only prize cared for by the powerful is power. The prize of the general is not a bigger tent, but command."

Here's the rule:

A company that allows the pursuit of personal power to substitute for true managerial leadership is doomed to perennial underachievement and, ultimately, complete failure.

This nation is on its way to being a powerful, hi-tech, Third World country. The people in places of leadership in our government, Fortune 50 companies, entertainers, and journalists want wealth, fame, and the power to determine the lives of everyone else. Look at how movie stars and other celebrities are pushing political agendas to dictate how our society acts. Stardom is not enough.

Look at the top executives who are snuggling up to the entertainment elite. Look at the top executives' pay packages, termination agreements, and retirement benefits.

But most important, look at how willing they are to seek their own aggrandizement at the expense of the company. Doing what is right for the company and the people who work there is now viewed as *noblesse oblige*. This mentality is making its way into the mid-tier companies. There are a few holdouts in the big companies, IBM being the notable example; Hewlett-Packard had a slip and is now struggling to get back on track. There are still many fine companies being managed superbly. But these are not the ones whose executives make the evening news as either scoundrels or media darlings.

The good news is that even in the most despotic nations on earth, if a company is run on the basis of *what* and not *how*, if the leaders view that as a sober and inviolable obligation and not noblesse oblige, then that company will do better than its competitors. To the extent it is possible to succeed, it will succeed.

Let's apply this new concept (which some of you will now claim you knew all along) to the first of two fundamental roles of a manager - personnel management. The next section will undoubtedly disturb a number of people who have lectured on the subject because Section 2 will actually deal mostly with real people in real situations. Normally, the only time I wouldn't use real people and real situations is when I want to look smarter than I really am. I couldn't figure out how to do that, so all you'll get is reality and my apologies to the academic[1] types.

I'll give those in academia some relief (but not much) in Section 3 when we talk about how to apply the what-versus-how principle to strategic, tactical, and operational management.

---

[1] I don't want to pick on business schools and professors too much. Somehow the USA with 5% of the world's population keeps doing pretty well in the commerce arena and a lot of it has to do with solid teaching in our MBA programs. The professors that drive me nuts and whose books are heavily hyped are often from some odd institute. I was forced to read their books. I still have bruises from the few times I tried applying what I read. I eventually learned to read stuff by guys who, like me, got bruised and *then* wrote books.

Section 2

Personnel Management

(And Management of Managers)

(And Managing Yourself, Come to Think of It)

Preface to the Subject of Personnel Management

Is there any profession, sport, or hobby where training in the fundamentals wouldn't make a big difference? Is there anyone entering into the profession of management who wouldn't benefit from some general guidelines and the experiences of others? Some people are natural leaders but even those who are (as opposed to overbearing taskmasters) need to learn the ropes. And as for overbearing taskmasters, they need both the fundamentals and a kick in the butt. The kick in the butt is not to wake them up or to get them going; it's because they deserve it and it makes *me* feel better about the universe.

The secret to successful personnel management is to surround yourself with the best people you can and then focus on performance, not what good or bad people they are.

There are three things that will make you successful:

1. Hiring capable people
2. Emphasizing *what* instead of *how*.
3. Dealing in business issues - not personalities.

Doing these three things will give you considerable control over the outcome of your business unit's endeavors. But you have to pick the right people and then you actually have to *know* what to do.

Most people are bosses (in the pejorative sense) and not managers. Most managers who are effective are also natural leaders but that is not a requirement. Management is a profession. Professional skills can be learned. Lack of leadership skill will probably, but not necessarily, prevent someone from reaching the upper echelons of a large corporation. However, all the way up the chain of command, executives are also managers, responsible for the cumulative results of the people who work for them. How you go about getting these results is the purpose of this section.

To emphasize the importance of professional training over natural talent, I'll give you a personal illustration in the field of sports.

About a year after high school I got a call from a former Roosevelt High classmate. I didn't know him very well. He was a bit of a quiet type and he didn't seem to have a lot of friends. I was one of those people who tried to treat everyone well. Wallflower types were very appreciative of that fact. I never shunned anybody. This is not the general M.O. of many people who have lots of friends and are doing well from a popularity standpoint.

My former classmate had an interesting request – one which I almost instinctively was ready to turn down. He asked if I would go with him and his family to Nathan Hale High School to play badminton.

Badminton?

He explained that there were people from all different countries there and it would be a lot of fun. For some reason, I agreed to go.

When I got to the gym, there were about a half dozen games going on. I had played badminton in my back yard and this did not look like the tap-tap, ping-ping games that we all used to play. It was amazingly fast and some of the people could drill that shuttlecock so hard I swear it broke the sound barrier. The Pakistanis were especially powerful players.

It became clear to all that I was a schlub. After a couple of games and dozens of patronizing remarks, it was suggested that I go to court 5 and play with Arnie. I looked over at court five and saw a man bending down, taking his racket out of its case. A case? Badminton rackets come in cases? That wasn't right. Badminton rackets are kept in garage corners or closets, not cases.

Arnie turned around and walked toward me, smiling. He was 74 and not in all that great a shape. It was humiliating that I had been sent down to babysit gramps. He asked me if I wanted to serve and I said, "Nah, you go ahead."

That was a mistake.

As you might suspect, I got my clock cleaned. What was worse, there were people watching. And even worse than that, they were cheering for me and saying little encouraging things like, "Oh, so close!" or "Oh, you almost got it, before that nosedive!" and "Just a couple more inches and it would have cleared the net."

It couldn't clear the net. I was tangled in the net! Arnie, the animal, kept doing this little underhanded, side-flicky thing that plopped the birdie about two inches on my side of the net. On the few occasions where I anticipated this (and I wasn't lying on the floor) I rushed the net, whereupon he did this little backhanded-flicky thing and the ball would go just high enough over my head to make me think I could reach up and swat it.

My turn. I was down 9 – 0 before I got a chance to serve. I had lost all sense of sportsmanship. This guy was old and I was determined to make him run on his arthritic knees. It was my only chance. I aimed for the corner. It turns out you have to whack it pretty hard to get the birdie into the corner. Birdies have this non-aerodynamic aspect that slows them down exponentially fast over a distance. Arnie flicked it back and then walked to the back line to start serving again. He didn't even look to see if he had won the shot. He could tell from the rapid squeak, squeak, squeak of my sneakers pawing desperately at the gymnasium floor that I was scrambling. The sound of "Naaargghhh," as I tangled in the net, confirmed my failure.

I lost 15-1.

Okay, so much for skill. Let's try badminton etiquette. Common sense stuff, right?

As I improved a little, a nice middle-aged couple asked me and my high school friend if we wanted to play a doubles game. I was excited because I had finally learned to smash the birdie. I had been watching the Pakistanis and I picked up the basic form. I was ready to use it.

Five points into the game, I was about six feet from the net and I was delivered an overhead opportunity the size of a cantaloupe. I whacked it. I whacked it *hard*! I felt the harmonic muscle feedback you get when you've hit the sweet spot on your racket. The shuttlecock whistled piercingly as it made its way perfectly across the net and right at the exposed skin on the woman's chest, just above the neckline of her blouse. Splat!

Instantly, little broken red capillaries radiated out in all directions from the point of impact. I had created on her formerly smooth white skin, a perfect replica of the Andromeda Galaxy. Several people rushed to her aid to see if I had broken her ribs or disconnected the cartilage along her sternum.

My friend looked over to me and said quietly, "Men typically don't do an overhead smash in mixed doubles."

I could hear a lot of murmuring. It wasn't clear what everyone was saying but I did pick out a few words. "Oaf!" "The man's a philistine!" I heard a man from Britain say, "He has the manners of a cannibal."

I was a varsity quarter-miler/half-miler in high school - one of the most promising in Seattle before my injuries sidelined me in my junior year. I had been a boxer, tennis player, and good wide receiver. When I was only 5'9" I could dunk a basketball. Without question, I was the best *natural* athlete on the floor.

Furthermore, I was raised in a good home, under strict English house rules. When a woman came to the dining table or stood up to leave, I stood as well. I brushed my teeth every single day. Yet on the badminton court I was a disaster. The snooty British guy was right. I was a cannibal.

I had no skills, no sense of what to do to turn around a progressively worse score and I had no sense of how to act in some of the social aspects because I just didn't know any better. Some things are intuitive and some can be absorbed through exposure. A whole lot of things can be taught. Imagine what twenty minutes of lessons and a couple of pointers on etiquette could have done for me – and for everyone else.

The woman I had hit had to change her entire wardrobe to include blouses and sweaters that button up to where her Adam's apple would be if women had an Adam's apple.

Most people enter management the same way and often have similar results in their first couple of years. Some never get invited back to the game. Lots of their employees are walking around with the psychological equivalent of the Andromeda Galaxy splattered onto their psyches.

At a well-known large software company, there was a feeling that if you hired really smart people, which they did, then all you had to do was give them lots and lots of room to operate and they would do great. In the 80s and 90s it was one of the most difficult places I have ever done business, in terms of rough treatment.

Smarts and more smarts do not a management culture make. The company mentioned above is a much better managed operation now but for a while it was flame-mails, nasty job interviews, and a degree of chaos brought on by rapid growth and an ambitious set of plans for the future, with too few curbs on behavior, in my judgment.

***

There's an old saying:

Good judgment comes from experience and experience comes from bad judgment.

Now let's see if we can make management more fun by avoiding too many "experiences."

Chapter Two
Universal Management Concepts

How many times have I been told that American management concepts wouldn't work in many other cultures? This remains true right up until the time we open up a business in the country in question and then it works just fine. True, you can't just fire up a business and then walk away but isn't that what management is all about? It assumes you're going to hang around and manage.

The only place I think *might* not adopt American-style management in general is the Middle East. It is still too oriented to the concept that one guy at the top gives all the orders.

So let's start with the basics.

Workers are human beings full of emotions, aspirations, character flaws, misconceptions, health problems and phenomenal potential. We have this sacrilegious tendency to believe that employees are to be created in our image – or at least our perception of our image.

There was a bumper sticker that came out years ago that I really liked. Although it has universal application beyond cars and driving, it's pretty good just for driving:

CAUTION, I DRIVE AS LOUSY AS YOU DO!

Remember, you're a manager, not because you're a better person; you're a manager because it is believed by the people who put you there that you have good management skills.

Here's something you might find kind of handy. I call it, somewhat modestly:

THE FIRST EVER UNIVERSAL JOB DESCRIPTION FOR EVERY EMPLOYEE ON EARTH

Many have tried to create such a job description. Until now, all have failed.

I have in the flat drawer of my desk, a photo of Albert Einstein trying to create a universal job description. In it he looks stressed; his hair is standing on end. In the background is a wastebasket full of little wadded up pieces of paper from prior failed attempts.

On the day he gave up he wrote in his diary, "Forget it. I'm going to see if time, matter and energy are somehow related."

Here is the job description that is true in any galaxy:

The job of an employee is to influence or control the flow of information to his or her boss.

That's it!

I use the generic term "boss" because this is for the whole universe and the majority of people in positions of authority over Earthlings and other humanoids are bosses, lacking almost entirely in management skills or inclination.

In the case of an employee working on the assembly line in a putty knife factory, the way information gets to the boss is pretty straightforward. If you assemble 375 putty knives, the boss will see that you assembled 375 putty knives.

In the case of a welder on the Alaskan Pipeline bringing oil from the North Slope, he welds so many welds in a given period of time and then they X-ray every single one. You can't just walk into the office and tell your boss you did a great job. You can't even get your friends to say that. The X-ray analysis tells him.

In the case of sales people, it would seem to be straightforward but it isn't. Yes, they get measured on units sold or revenue generated. But they can control the flow of information in terms of how customers feel, how hard it is to sell in their particular patch, the prevalence of competition and how good they're doing fighting it off.

The more white-collar the job, the more control the employee has over what gets to his or her boss. This gets us back to managing on the one or two most salient issues. (See the two hoops strategy in Chapter 10). All the other stuff is secondary. As soon as the employee is in control not only of what gets to you via his or her performance, but also how you should view it and how the various elements should be valued, you are no longer the manager, he or she is. You are the administrator, hoping it all works out.

The closer you can get even complex, brainy, gaseous, ephemeral jobs down to measurements similar to the pipeline welder, the better. They will still influence the flow of information, but it will be via direct, desired output and not solely through fluff, hearsay and great internal PowerPoint presentations.

What you're really aiming for is something that is ultimately more humane. If you can get the employee into a position where you and the employee can look objectively at what's going on, without the employee being defensive, then the two of you are solving a business problem together. Performance becomes this object that sits on the table and the two of you look at it, analyze it and make decisions about it. You ask her, "What do you think about this area?" And she says, "I think that part's okay, but I want to focus more on this area in the next round." And you say, "Do you have the resources you need to pull that off?" And she says, "Let me look at my existing pipeline and I'll get back to you. I may need some more help."

There, wasn't that pleasant? It's like you're both from the same planet, you both have belly buttons and you both count the number of items in the basket of the guy in front of you when you're in the express checkout lane at the supermarket. We are people long before we become employees - or even managers.

The next thing you may want to do is get a forecast and then have the same kind of discussion. Ask how realistic it is to expect to deliver products when the order comes in toward the end of the quarter. Maybe she has an answer. Maybe she needs to get more orders well ahead of that. What will that take in order to get it done? She needs to tell you. You need to decide if she has it under control and then you need to follow up if it's important and time critical. You and she just need to agree on when would be a good time for her to give you an update. She recommends; you accept or edit.

Employees will appreciate it and you will be compared to considerably fewer human body parts than the average manager.

Does that mean you can't be personal about things? I hope that's not what it means. I care deeply about the people who work for me. I talk about all kinds of stuff with them. We'll talk about the pitfalls of being "one of the gang" a little later in the book. But being a member of the human race does not cross the line.

I care so deeply about most of the people who report to me that I don't want to whipsaw them back and forth emotionally, based on what they *think* I think of them. I want them to know what I think of their performance. And I want them to know that their performance determines, pay, position and on rare occasions, job security.

Let' look at a good example:

When I went to work at STAR, a 700-person systems integration firm where I eventually became CEO, I was the Seattle VP and General Manager for a time. I wanted the salespeople to report directly to me. This was not a big change for them because prior to that, they had reported to Sid Christiansen, one of the owners.

One of the salespeople was a woman we'll call Betty Sue. She was a good salesperson but she had a lot of nasty habits. One of them was keeping secrets when she should have come and talked to me. She and a recruiter, we'll call Belinda, had responsibility for a good sized account with a lot of our people billing pretty high revenues.

Betty Sue called Belinda one day and let her know that a shakeup had been going on for some time and that a number of billable people were going to be coming off the account. Belinda said, "We have to tell Charles." Betty Sue wanted to wait. She waited. Things got worse.

At 4:00 one afternoon, Belinda came to see me. She said she thought there *might be* a problem. I asked why and she said that a half dozen people were getting laid off at the end of the week and that was just the start of it. Betty Sue had not wanted to tell me because she was about to leave on vacation and she didn't want to be bugged about it while she was off trying to have fun.

Someone told Betty Sue that Belinda had come to see me. Betty Sue showed up whirling around like the Tasmanian Devil at about 5:30 PM, hearing that I had gone home. She pounded on Belinda's door and yelled, for all to hear, "Get out here, you (adjective for common but atrocious expletive having to do with human interaction) + (noun for common but atrocious expletive having to do with canine gender distinction).

The pounding went on for a while because Belinda had also gone home.

Of course, the next day, everyone had heard about it. Betty Sue was nowhere to be found so I gave her a call. She came to my office and I asked what had happened. She told me, fully expecting bad things to now happen to her. I did not need to tell her she had done something wrong. I just asked her what she was going to do to clean up the mess. She explained both her business plan and her personal plan to talk to the people who had witnessed the affair.

She asked me what I was going to do. I told her essentially that every dog gets a free bite unless it's really a bad bite. This was close but not quite bad enough. I asked her what she would do in my situation. She was kind of stuck. I had another good question. What would have happened if Belinda had opened her door? That one hit home.

Her former boss, Sid Christiansen had, like everyone else, heard all about the event. He asked to see me. I told him I had already handled it and that I doubted she would do it again. He then slid a piece of paper across the desk for me to look at. It was Betty Sue's annual appraisal form. Her appraisal was due the next day and he had failed to tell me (and I had failed to ask). He asked if I wanted to put it off until after she came back from vacation. I said that this was a perfect opportunity to make a point on management. He didn't like the sound of that. So he asked me what I planned to do about her appraisal.

"I plan to give her high rankings on her sales performance and talk to her a bit about her forecasts and some other territory management items but for the most part it would be a good appraisal. I let him know that although I wouldn't talk about pay in an appraisal, she also had a raise coming in the next month or so and she would get it."

He stopped by my office on his way home and said how relieved he was that I was not going to make this a personal thing. Betty Sue had not been a very big supporter of mine and she had run off at the mouth about me a couple of times and he knew it. I told him I was playing this for the long run and I wasn't going to let one incident wipe out an entire year's work on her part.

"Sid, she will likely never be a huge fan of mine. But she'll come around."

"You know what I think it is," Sid said, scratching his head. "I think she just got a little too big for her britches."

"I think she just misbehaves horribly and it has nothing to do with britches. She has shown a lack of self-control on other occasions from what I have heard. She needs to fix it."

At the end of Betty Sue's appraisal meeting, I waited for the look of shock to wear off and then I told her again what a great job she had done. Then I had to deal with the elephant in the living room.

"Here's the bad spot you've put me in, Betty Sue. I believe that you've done a great job and I am doing a very professional thing by separating last night from last year. Unfortunately, all those people out there will simply view this as a case that if your sales are good enough, you can do anything you want. Is that the kind of message you think should be sent to the congregation at large?"

She saw the predicament. She had a suggestion. "You could tell them that I'm on probation and that one more time like the other night and it won't go so well."

"I don't discuss personnel actions with other employees. It's none of their business," I explained flatly.

We both sat quietly for a bit. She finally said to me, "There's no good answer for this situation is there?"

"That's right, Betty Sue. You have put me in a situation where there is no good answer."

She started to apologize and I held up my hand. I continued. "There's no good answer, but there is a *right* answer. The right answer is for both of us to play this game for the long run. You have to change your habits. You have to be more pleasant and forgiving. You have to quit badmouthing other people, including me. And I have to go about the business of getting this company turned around. I don't have time for this kind of thing and I won't be as patient next time. In the meantime, we're both going to look a little punkie for a bit."

That's just the way it is. Sometimes there is no satisfying or clean answer. Sometimes there is no immediate relief. Lots of times, you don't get to go out and tell everyone why you did what you did. And you can never say why you didn't publically punish someone who deserved it. Sometimes it just hurts and it isn't fair.

Sometimes doing the right thing creates a bit of a mess. Do it anyway.

I separated her performance from my personal feelings, for the most part. Every dog does get a free bite. I didn't defend my position to the world because it was between me and her. I also made it clear to Betty Sue and many other people over the first several months of my tenure that this was going to be a more professional company

Reputations take a long time to build, so just keep doing the right things and you'll get there.

But isn't there this nagging sense that the whole thing with the account and the big blowup should have cost her more?

Sometime after she came back from vacation, we reviewed the account in question. She had failed in her job as the company steward of that account. She also did not have a good get-well plan. For *both* reasons the account was taken away from her. It was therefore taken away because I no longer believed she was the best person to manage that account - not because I was angry or because of one incident. That incident and her relationship with the recruiter factored in but they were not the primary determining factors. When she lost the account, everyone understood, including her. Some say that she lost the account because of the big expletive explosion that day. Some say she lost it because it got away from her. You decide. But with patience…

Eventually, it all works out.

Just a couple of other management pointers here: The day after the big expletive explosion, I had her into my office. How did I start off the meeting? This is important. I didn't do what 99% of all managers would do. We'll talk about what that was in just a moment.

The other pointer: I took care of everything prior to her going on vacation and allowed her to leave without a sense of dread. Keep in mind, when an employee takes his or her vacation, they need to have a break. They shouldn't be worrying about their job security. Their kids need to have mom or dad thinking of them. Kids grow up fast and then you never have those moments again where you can be out at Yellowstone or Disneyland and just have a magical time. Let your employees have that break and don't leap on them when they come back. In fact, don't ever leap on them.

Here's a great rule that I can't take credit for:

Treat others the way you would want to be treated

Before I replay the Betty Sue discussion the day after the explosion, let's see if you can pass the test that almost all managers in my training classes fail. It will answer the earlier question about what I *didn't* do. Here's the situation:

You are a manager in a large consulting firm. You have a ten million dollar deal on the table at Big Bank, Inc. There is one thing you know for a fact, the people at Big Bank probably need your company but they really don't like your company.

Progress has been made and now a critical meeting has been called to discuss the final presentation. Reluctantly, some of the Big Bank employees have agreed to meet and preview your presentation. Jacob, the person you have given primary responsibility to for Big Bank will take them through the well thought out set of slides.

You have been sitting in this somewhat hostile environment now for 20 minutes, waiting for Jacob to show up. The nasty remarks start coming your way. A couple of people leave in disgust. Finally, after 45 minutes, you cancel the meeting. Everyone leaves without any offer to reschedule. It is a long drive home.

You leave a message on Jacob's cell phone to come see you first thing in the morning.

It's 8 AM. Jacob is at your door. You motion for him to come in and take a seat. You start the conversation. What do you say?

Think about it. He may have just lost the company a ten million dollar deal. In addition, you were personally humiliated. A lot of employees were counting on you and Jacob to get this deal so there would be enough work at a fairly slow time. This was critical.

So, once again, how do you start this conversation?

Here's how most people start it in the management class:

"Jacob! I sat there for 45 minutes waiting for you for a critical meeting. Those people hate us and you gave them even more reason to hate us. We waited forty five minutes! *Why* were you late?!!!"

During the role play, I take on the character of Jacob. As soon as they ask me the big question: "*Why* were you late?!" I respond:

"You ask me why. I don't know. I guess when I was a kid and there was a big issue going on, my dad was pretty hard on me. He would say, 'Jacob, get in here. I want to have a *word* with you!' It wasn't easy. I wet my bed until I was 12. My dog died and I think it might have been me that killed him by feeding him snail pellets instead of kibble. You know, sometimes it's really hard to get up in the morning. On weekends I don't comb my hair and lots of times I just eat over the sink. Do you want me to keep going?"

Totally confused, the management class student usually just stares at me. So I keep going.

"Do you ever think of just not stopping when the light turns red? I mean..."

I usually let other people in the class try a shot at Jacob but inevitably they make the same mistake. They demand that Jacob explain himself to them.

Your question is "Why?" My question for you then is: How deeply psychoanalytical do you want to get?

Jumping right to my troubled childhood doesn't sound like the natural flow to you? Actually, I'm just saving us the two to six hours it takes to get there. When people are defending their jobs, they feel like their life is being threatened. They will do anything they think will work. This inevitably includes pulling out the personal problems that they hope (and expect) you to take into consideration. The bigger the trouble they are in, the more likely it is that you will know marital, spiritual, and digestive tract issues you probably aren't ready to discuss. Do you really want to put another human being into that position? It's not nice.

Yes, it seems very natural to want to ask someone in this circumstance why the #@!!$ they were late. But like most professions, you need to act counter-intuitively. That's what makes you a professional. Think of any sport you ever learned. Didn't they ask you to do things that just didn't feel natural? Yet, once you did them, you did well; and afterwards you couldn't imagine doing it any other way. Think how a soldier feels when the bullets are flying. But if a group of soldiers wants to win a battle, they have to go counter to their *feelings* and execute.

Sure, asking someone *why* the heck they were late or *why* the heck they didn't show up seems natural. But it's better to do it like a pro, even with the small things like being late or somewhat bigger things like going nuclear in the office like Betty Sue did. It allows you to create a professional basis for what may be a very long and tough conversation. So do it.

> Here's the rule:
> **Never ask an adult to explain himself or herself to another adult.**

It's probably not a great idea for anyone to make someone explain themselves, including kids over the age of 4. However, there can be a discussion and questions can get asked and answered.

Back to Jacob. Try this approach and see how it feels.

You pleasantly offer Jacob a seat and then you begin.

"Jacob, yesterday's meeting was important. I had to cancel it when it was pretty clear you weren't going to show up. That's not like you. What happened?"

The difference between asking "*Why* did you...?!" and "What happened?" is significant. It is the difference between "Explain yourself!" and "Let's talk about it." I'm not being 1970's groovy here. I just want to get down to business, figure out what happened and then move on to the solution phase. It will be a lot easier to do that with someone who doesn't feel like he has to defend himself or who doesn't feel like he's being treated like one of the cogs in someone else's machine.

Right now, while no one is looking, ask the "why did you" question out loud and see if you can make it sound good. No matter how you do it, no matter what sing-songy voice you employ or condescending smile you add, you cannot ask that question and talk straight across to another human being. But you can ask another human being in the most collegial manner, "What happened?" This simple and ostensibly subtle difference in your approach and the thinking behind it, will determine whether you get to talk about performance or you get to deal in personal issues. It will determine whether you are a manager or whether you are just a boss.

The above example with Jacob was from a class I ran at STAR. When I came to STAR, there was no management culture. There were owners looking at spreadsheets and people doing stuff. So I crammed 16 years of IBM training into a one-day management class. It made a huge difference. People just needed a model for their thinking as opposed to a million rules or something formulaic like the popular books coming out at the time – and for the prior twenty to thirty years.

But something must have been sitting in my subconscious, waiting to get out because I had a situation very similar to the one with Jacob, mentioned above. I'll put it in context because the context is kind of an interesting story too.

I had taken a job at IBM to hold me until I went to medical school. I was one of 228 pre-screened applicants for one opening in Seattle for a large systems "marketing rep." It was toward the end of the stagflation era ushered in by Jimmy Carter, perhaps the worst president in American history. I say "perhaps" because I really haven't studied up that much on Millard Fillmore (1850-1853). But I'm thinking Fillmore gets the edge just by not being Jimmy Carter.

In the applicant mix there were Ivy League and Stanford MBA's, people with Masters Degrees in Computer Science, etc. I had great grades but I had no idea what a computer looked like. I also did not realize that "marketing" was IBM's term for sales. Yuk. I had tried to walk out of my first interview but they lured me back with IBM's famous Data Processing Aptitude tests. I love tests and I aced it. Now there were only 10 applicants.

I believe I got the job because I was the most arrogant. I really didn't want a sales job so I kept pushing them to tell me why I should come to work there. "I have other options," I explained like a little snot. I also had a scholarship offer to law school. A friend of mine who was a pre-law student knew that I liked tests so he talked me into paying the $35 dollars to take the LSAT (Law School Admission Test). I showed up at his house at 7 AM and he came to the door, bleary-eyed and told me he wasn't going to go because he hadn't studied enough. I was shocked, not because he wasn't going to go. He was always backing out of things. I was shocked because I didn't know you could study for the test. He showed me a three inch book with a big American flag on the front, titled appropriately, *Barron's Guide to the LSAT*. I took the test anyway and scored so high I got a scholarship offer when I applied to Law School. It was my backup plan if I couldn't get into medical school.

I needed to kill 18 months so I went to work for IBM and was immediately whisked away to New York, off and on, for weeks at a time for 18 months of intense technical and marketing training. This prevented me from taking the medical college admission test. Gruesomely, I was going to have to, yuk, sell something. Fortunately, I was in the DP division which only sold big expensive systems, so there wasn't really any meretricious or *salesy* stuff.

For my territory, I was to replace a person who was about to be promoted to the San Francisco region. So, in the meantime, they gave me a "practice sales patch" for the six month period until he left. But he didn't leave. He screwed up and all of a sudden, the practice patch was a real patch where I was actually supposed to *sell* something. The customer accounts were back-level, non-growing insurance companies with machines that were at least 10 years old. All the accounts had two things in common besides being in the insurance industry: They loved their old equipment and they totally despised IBM.

My manager knew I couldn't survive in that territory, so he added King County Medical/Blue Shield. They more or less fit the profile. They were in the insurance industry and they despised IBM. But they were different from the other insurance companies in one respect. They planned to upgrade from their old IBM equipment. Unfortunately, they planned to upgrade to an Amdahl and not an IBM mainframe. This is the only reason the crafty old IBM rep prior to me had been willing to give it up. (See my rule on people willingly giving up accounts or employees of value in Chapter 11).

They had assigned to me as my systems engineer, a woman named Debra. She was inexperienced, just like me. And she wasn't a very hard worker. This did not cause the client to hate her any worse than they hated me. They couldn't. The hate meter was pegged in the red-purple zone the minute I walked in the door. My being a natural smartass didn't help me any.

One of the technical issues being discussed was the fact that IBM's VM operating system ran faster on an Amdahl then it did on an IBM mainframe. As an IBMer, I had to point out to the client the obvious drawbacks of having a competitive machine running our software better than we could run it. (Insert Alfred E. Neuman look here). I scheduled a technical rebuttal meeting for 3 PM on a Wednesday. The Amdahl was a faster processor but at some point it had to go out and get data off disk drives, pull things in and out of virtual memory, talk to other software, talk to telecom control systems, etc. They were bringing more and applications online, which would require much more input/output device interaction and the ability to run our CICS (communication control) software.

41

We had some advantages that we had to hop on. The people who hated us would brush these facts aside. Remember, it's just like political affiliation these days. In fact, it's almost a religion and you are not going to change sides no matter what facts or logic are presented and proved. If people want to hate you, they will likely continue to find reasons to hate you. But in this case, if they couldn't _counter_ our claims, then we could point that out when we went forward for the next leg of the sales process - financial justification.

We sat in the I-hate-IBM meeting for about fifteen minutes, waiting for Debra. She was uncharacteristically late. IBMers were never late. Twenty minutes of sitting ushered in a new topic: Why IBM was such a horrible company. People all around the table had war stories from past dealings with IBM. None of them were nice stories. It left me wondering how Hitler was able to invade Poland to start the Second World War before IBM got there. I had no idea IBM had both bombed Pearl Harbor and led the effort on Japanese internment in America. Despite not having a history degree, I felt those actions were at cross-purposes with one another

At 45 minutes, we all agreed the meeting was over. The VP of MIS and Chief IBM Hater told me there was no need to reschedule. I took that as a bad sign.

I went back to the office and waited until 6 o'clock for Debra. She didn't show up.

The next morning I chewed Debra out. I told her what a lousy systems engineer she was and how she had no sense of marketing. I explained that there was no further need for technical support at this point since the sales effort was now purely a financial issue, pitting our machine against a system that was faster and 30% less expensive, in an environment where having IBM support was viewed as a negative. I

42

stomped away from my meeting with Debra without really hearing her out. I never felt so right in my life.

So, what had caused Debra to be late? She had parked in a parking garage and when she came back to her car, someone had parked their car behind hers and she couldn't get out. The other guy's car was still running but the door was locked. She waited, thinking the owner of the car would come back. After 20 minutes, she went and got help. For the next 30 minutes, the tow truck company worked to get the mystery car's door open. When they finally did, she hurried to our meeting which was over by the time she got there. She actually got back to the office before I did but when she saw I wasn't there, she went home.

All I had to do was ask a simple question: What happened?

Things were never good between Debra and me after that. She wasn't a very good systems engineer and she knew it. She knew one other thing: This Charles Herrick guy that everyone thought was so personable could really be a jerk. I could claim that I didn't have the management training that would have taught me to ask "What happened" instead of "Why did you screw up, Mrs. Screw-up?" But the truth is, all that would have accomplished is to give me the correct alternative to the latter. I still could have been civil.

As a side note, the competitive battle was far from over. I found a friend in the Chief Financial Officer. My presentation to him, the President, and the VP of MIS (Chief IBM Hater) went surprisingly well. It was surprising because the VP of MIS had not done his homework. He showed how much higher the cost was on the IBM than the Amdahl. And while it was true, he acknowledged, there were higher ongoing expenses with the Amdahl, they would in no way make up for the fact that the price tag of the IBM machine was so much higher.

My argument was that since this was a non-profit corporation, they were simply trading a cash asset for an equipment asset and therefore the <u>only</u> financial measurement should be expense. Not bad for a pre-med guy. They didn't teach me *that* in organic chemistry.

I threw in a bunch of other stuff along with some FUD (Fear, Uncertainty and Doubt about not using IBM). We won.

The VP of MIS and I had to work together for another year before I was put on the Safeco account. He pointed out that I didn't do the customary things that other marketing people did such as big dinners, trips and football games. I told him he was not a very nice person and I didn't think it would be very much fun to do those kinds of things with him. Remember, I was going to go to medical school, so I really didn't care what he thought. In my entire career, I made it a point never to go out for business lunches on any kind of regular basis – and certainly not with people I didn't like.

The people who did come to like me were the seven other insurance accounts. John Simpson, VP of a mid-size, Seattle-based life insurance company, and I became friends and we went to lunch together - a lot. We both loved cheesecake and we spent one winter trying to figure out which restaurant in Seattle had the best cheesecake. Note: El Gaucho's restaurant won, but we never told them. Maybe Mr. Gaucho will read this book and feel requited.

John wasn't going to order a system from me because his company had been bought by a very large Midwest insurance company. The new owners were tough guys and he wasn't about to suddenly raise his profile by spending lots of money.

I came back to him after he told me that and said, "John, you feel that your back is up against a cliff and you're kind of making your way forward very carefully as you sort out the situation with the company that now owns your company." He agreed. I then said, "I actually don't see your situation as even that good. I think you're more like on a tightrope. True, you can't spend a ton of money but at the same time, the company that acquired you is a big believer in the benefits of technology – and new IBM technology at that. I checked. They're going to ask you what you're doing to make the company more efficient and productive with information technology. Isn't that your job?"

I then handed John the same analysis I had shown him a month prior which proved that our new system was so inexpensive to operate and maintain, and that the computer and all the peripherals would require so little electricity and air-conditioning, that there would be virtually no net expense increase. It all of a sudden sounded good to him. To allow him to save face I completely reformatted it. And I used a different color paper.

Did you notice something? He bought the machine based on what it would do for his job security, not for the fact that it would allow his company to remain competitive. That's how it works. Play into it or be a starving philosopher.

SIDEBAR
The "Only" Rule in Business
Fatherly (-in law) Advice

My father-in-law was a solid businessman. He was smart and tough and honorable. In the commercial real estate world he had a reputation as "someone you could do business with"; a rather pedestrian statement but possibly the best appellation you could hope for in business. His name was Jack Davidson

He co-developed a fairly large shopping mall called Factoria Square, just outside Seattle, along with several other retail centers up and down the I-5 corridor and throughout the Puget Sound region. His reputation grew with each deal. And he loved his work. He felt I should forget going to med school and get into the real estate business.

So when Jack found out that I was going to work for IBM, he was ecstatic. He didn't know that I still planned to go to medical school. At the end of my first month he invited me over to his office in the Park Place building across the street to give me the facts of life regarding the business world. I still remember the conversation almost word for word because I have repeated it often to others. It was a valuable talk, giving me an important perspective. Here's how it went. Did I mention he's a very direct (as in blunt) individual?

"Charles, I'm glad to hear you got rid of that stupid idea of going to medical school. You need to be out in the real world doing business. IBM is a good place to start. Medical School would have been a waste of your talent."

"How so?" I asked, thinking back on four years of organic chemistry, calculus and microbiology.

"Because you're a peddler, just like me."

"I never thought of myself as a peddler, mostly because I have never actually peddled anything."

"Well, you are. You're a peddler. And that's where all the money is." He then launched into a soliloquy he had prepared just for me, the husband of his only daughter.

"Now, I know you go to church and you believe in the Golden Rule and the Ten Commandments and all that lovey religious stuff that feels good. But out here there's only one rule and here it is: you keep your commitments. Now, you're young and sometimes young people are stupid and they make commitments to things they ought not to have. Keep 'em anyway! Over time, you'll wise up and be a bit more circumspect when you agree to do something. But no matter what, you keep your commitments. Otherwise, you'll be known as a guy who doesn't stand by his word and that is death in business."

In my opinion, Jack's "one rule in business" and the Ten Commandments, Golden Rule and all that lovey stuff are not necessarily mutually exclusive. I've tried hard to keep them all, with about the same less-than-perfect success as everyone else who has tried to do so in the last 2,000 years. But Jack's statement stuck with me. I'm sure it's a codicil to those others, or at least a corollary. But if you don't think about it – if you don't keep it at the forefront of your operating philosophy, then it can remain a hidden corollary and it comes back to haunt you. It's not *hidden* from the other guy.

Jack died just as I took over the helm at STAR. He wasn't there when my career started to take off. I could have used his insights and his sincere counsel. He and I had a special relationship. He told me things, such as his time spent as a tail-gunner on a B-24 in the South

Pacific during World War II. He had never told anyone else and after hearing them, I understand why. Often, as in the case of a side-gunner on Jack's bomber who never cleaned his 50mm, he got to see people get hurt and killed by others not keeping their commitments, spoken or implied. It was a big thing to him. It became a big thing to me. I told him so in the last days of his battle with mesothelioma, an asbestos related disease he picked up working in the naval shipyards at the start of the war.

In the hospital when he and I were all alone, he came back out of a morphine-induced stupor and spoke absolutely lucidly for the first time in two days. I told him what we were about to do and that this would be his last day. He didn't' flinch. He took my hand and asked me to promise that I would take care of his 95 year old mother, his wife, and his daughter – my wife Kristy. He knew that I believed in the near sanctity of commitment and that it was either a part of your makeup or it wasn't.

He died a few hours later, assured that the three women in his life were in good hands – committed hands.

Chapter Three
Running For Homecoming Queen

Watching a manager dig himself out of the hole he has created by trying to be everyone's pal is pretty gruesome. It should have at least an R-rating.

Here's your first basic rule on this subject:

It's way easier to go from being an S.O.B to a pretty decent guy who is tough at times, than it is to go from being a sweetheart to a pretty decent guy who is tough at times.

When crunch time comes and you've been Mr. Nice Guy, you'll find you are lacking the key ingredient you need most: respect. You can't have respect as a leader unless you've got a few sharp teeth in your mouth that you're willing to use if you need them.

Let me give you two literary examples:

In the 1830s, a Harvard student signed up for duty on a merchant ship. His name was Richard Henry Dana and he wrote the book *Two Years before the Mast*. (Sailors slept in the area down below, just in front of the mast). He sailed from Massachusetts, around the tip of South America and up the California coast. The captain was a truly vicious man who had them working all the time, fixing this, cleaning that, tightening those, etc. He also flogged slackers on a regular basis.

When they got to California, they came alongside one of the company's sister ships. That ship needed some extra hands for the miserable task of scraping hides prior to tanning. Despite how horrible the job was, Richard was so hoping to get away from his captain that he volunteered. He had a time of bliss. The new captain was so pleasant, as was the new first mate. The crew was clearly much happier.

They headed out to sea one afternoon and several miles off the coast, they ran into a horrendous storm. The ship wasn't in that great a shape and they never did the drills that the beast captain had the other ship perform. The men were scrambling, each trying to figure out what to do. Somehow they survived. The problem was that the nice captain didn't have the skills to command, so he made up for it by being a nice guy. When it got tough, he didn't have their respect. They wouldn't listen to him and they looked to one guy after another for leadership. Richard was glad to get back on board his original ship. Fun's fun but he needed to live long enough to get back to Harvard.

I've seen this several times in business. I remember being in a team meeting for a major systems sale up in Alaska. It was a big bank and the IBM team was pitching a solution that was at about a million dollar disadvantage. I was brought in from San Francisco to assist.

The marketing manager was a weakling and the saleswoman was one tough character. We would go over possible strategies in an open format. Each time the marketing manager would say something, despite how reasonable it seemed to me, the team wouldn't even respond.

I talked to him afterward and asked him about the lack of civility. He didn't understand it either. He said, "When I came here I knew that I was going to be viewed as an outsider by all the Alaskans. I did everything I could to fit in and they just treated me worse and worse – especially Candace, the lead marketing rep."

He had done everything he could to fit in. How's that for an epitaph?

On the other end of that spectrum is the boss that says, "I don't get ulcers, I give ulcers!"

Somewhere in between is the right answer; but it's a bit closer to the ulcer guy when you're first starting. How about this as the right position if you show up as a new manager in a hostile environment: I don't normally get ulcers; but if I do get one, it won't be as big as yours. I'll be taking Tums while you're swallowing cement to plug the hole in your stomach lining."

If you're any good, you will never have to say this.

I mentioned there were two literary examples. Here's the other one:

Herman Wauk, the author of the *Cain Mutiny*, and *Winds of War*, etc. wrote a book in the 50s called *Marjorie Morningstar*. It was about a Jewish girl (Morgenstern is German for morning star) who wanted to become an actress and who also wanted to get married. She wasn't doing so great on either front.

She said to an older advisor one day that what she wanted in a husband was essentially a 100% nice guy. To this the older man responded by telling her that is *not* what she wanted. If you get a guy who isn't just a little bit of an S.O.B., he won't have the necessary nastiness to stand up against a nasty world. When they run him over, you'll get flattened right along with him.

Good managers can still be nice guys. I know lots of them. But they aren't using the nice guy shtick to get their employees to like them and do their bidding.

Every once in a while, I will encounter an employee or manager who has been used to running over people. I am generally pretty polite and friendly during first meetings. However, people who roll over people have a tendency to take advantage of polite and friendly people - people like me. The minute I see that, I usually make a very short speech: "Don't confuse kindness with weakness." That's terse and effective.

The goal is to get business down to where it's mostly business. The problem is there are still some human instincts that get in the way. As a species, we are pretty tough on weak leaders. Those in the distant past who put up with weaklings, cowards and the generally incompetent, didn't do such a good job at surviving long enough to have kids, let alone raise them to have more kids.

Whether we like a boss or not, most of us realize we are stuck with him or her. At the very least, we want to be able to respect our boss.

Here's a good question: Respect your boss for what? Looks, charm, smarts, technical prowess? Too often, managers believe they have to be the best at everything in order to have the respect of everyone. You just have to be a good leader and a disciplined manager. Everything after that is gravy.

So let's start with a really big rule for how to conduct yourself as a manager:

NEVER RUN FOR HOMECOMING QUEEN!

You will lose, even though you are the only one in the contest. When Earthlings detect you are trying to justify your authority based on them liking you, they know you're a liability. This is because if your authority depends on your popularity and for whatever reason you become unpopular, they will be without an effective leader. And if _you_ know your authority depends on your popularity, then you aren't going to jeopardize it by making tough, unpopular decisions. To illustrate how to use this rule, let's look at how I delivered one of the first big decisions I made at STAR Consulting:

As I have already mentioned, STAR was not a great place from a morale standpoint when I got there. When low morale occurs, people start looking out for themselves and to heck with a group they don't feel close to.

I made the rounds and talked to a lot of the internal staff to get their view of things. You almost never have to ask, "What do you think we should do differently?" They'll tell you. Then you get to decide how much of what they recommend is for the benefit of the company and how much of it is self-serving. In the case of all the STAR internal staff, it was approaching 90% self-serving.

Even though we were in a vicious war with other companies to garner the top technical talent, each of the five recruiters felt I should get rid of at least one recruiter. This would increase their commissions by 25%. Since this was the only real reason, and you couldn't actually make up another reason for running short of recruiters, they came up with a solution for making such a recommendation. They pointed out that person X was not very good. Purportedly the people that X hired tended to be poor fits for the jobs they were put onto. The interesting thing was that each of them identified a different person X. They perhaps were unaware that they were all at one point or another, a person X themselves.

When I talked to Lloyd, the founder, about recruiting, he too wanted me to cut back one recruiter in order to save money. I guess when you can't grow the top line, you cut costs using a dull meat cleaver, if necessary – or even if it's not necessary, come to think of it, according to his philosophy.

I then went to the field managers to get their perspective on things. The field managers were made up of two tiers. The internal tier was made up of staff managers. They were the ones who went out and did the official appraisals on our work force and gave raises. Their measurement was something that was shocking to me: They were measured on how many appraisals they did on time. If an appraisal was due August 10 and the staff manager did it August 10 or earlier then he had done his job. At each appraisal, the employee expected a raise. So they were appraising and pay-raising in the same meeting. This is never allowed in well-run companies.

The next tier was on-site field managers who were actually out on project doing billable assignments themselves. They were on our larger accounts and the employees could go to them with concerns, grievances, input, etc. they were like union supervisors. The company was always the bad guy. The on-site field managers never, ever took the company's position into consideration.

I had one meeting with them. They were howlers and harpies, demanding fixes right on the spot, no questions permitted. Despite their nastiness, I asked a lot of questions. It was clear they were doing more harm than good. I disbanded that group. I don't believe in supervisors anyway and I certainly don't believe in nasty, anti-company supervisors. They each had been receiving $2/hour on top of their regular pay. This meant that each of them made four thousand dollars per year just for showing up and collecting rotten things to say about STAR. There were 25 of them.

Those field managers snotting off saved STAR $100,000 per year!

Supervisors are a hybrid. They are not the actual manager but they have some say. Since they really can't hire and fire they employ a number of techniques to exercise power. Being the hero who fixes the evil corporate management team is one way to make people turn to you. You can have a team leader on a specific project but don't have people who perform managerial supervision without full authority.

Here's the rule on hybrids:

When you combine a management and a non-management role, the hybrid looks like the backside of both.

56

After recruiters and field managers came the final group - the sales group. These were the highest paid people in the company and they ruled the roost. I had been gathering input from them slowly, mostly about account status. I wanted to know how secure our revenue streams were, so I was holding account reviews.

I had started at STAR in September. By late October, Sid Christiansen, the former manager for the salespeople, called me in and asked me what my plan was for assigning next year's quotas. He thought the new quotas should be out by late November. I agreed on the timing and asked if he had any suggestions or if there were any things I should factor into my calculations. I was actually looking forward to this. I hadn't assigned quotas to salesmen since I was a first-line manager almost 15 years prior.

He felt that I should aim for about a 10% increase in the number of people billing. I sat back down and stared at him. I asked, "So, you want Betty Sue to go from 60 consultants billing in January to 66 billing by December 31st? That's about a half of a person added per month."

"It's not as easy as it seems, Charles," he responded a little briskly. "This isn't IBM, you know." I was reminded of that often. Just to piss people off I wore a pin stripe suit and a white shirt every day, even though I didn't even do that at IBM in my last years there.

"I don't see what IBM has to do with any of this."

"We don't have several layers of staff to help a salesman manage all the people out in the field," he pointed out.

"IBM didn't either. And speaking of lots of staff, I got rid of all the field managers the other night. Now there are even fewer 'levels of staff' to manage all the employees out in the field."

Sid was getting irritated. As one of the former owners, he was used to making just about every decision in council with the other owners and here I was just fixing things all by myself like I was being paid to do. He composed himself.

"Well then, Charles, how many new consultants should Betty Sue have billing by year end?"

"I think she should go from 60 to 90," I tossed out, casually. "Maybe a hundred."

"Somehow" that got leaked out and the salespeople were ready to storm the Bastille. So I called a meeting, not because of the threat of them storming the Bastille, but because I wanted to give them something to storm the Bastille about. They felt they had a *cause célèbre*[2] and I wanted them to have a *raison d'être*[3]. I was looking forward to this meeting. Here's how it went:

I gathered all the internal staff in a big room and laid out how we were going to be organized next year. I pointed out that our growth that year had been flat and that I expected that to change dramatically. When it did, everyone would be happy and make a lot of money. But things would have to change. I turned first to the salespeople. "I know it's great to have 60 or more people reporting to you so that when you go to a party you can tell people you have a big organization. But when we leave here today, you will have no one reporting to you. This means you'll be selling instead of wiping noses. And your quotas will be in the range of increasing your billable headcount by 50%, since you'll have so much free time.

---

[2] cause célèbre means: a notorious incident or episode, in this case, it was the incident of me dumping their comfortable but unprofitable organization over on their heads. Whereas...

[3] raison d'être means: reason or justification for existence. So they wanted to storm the Bastille and I wanted them to give me a reason they should show up for work and get paid as much as they were getting paid. Shades of Victor Hugo and Alexandre Dumas, Père. Oui? Non? N'est ce pas?

"Now, it should be pretty clear to you recruiters that we will need you to hire a lot more people so the salespeople can make their quotas. I know each of you has an opinion on the number of recruiters we need but since we're taking this new route to increasing sales, we're going from 5 of you to 12 and probably a recruiting manager to boot.

I then turned to the Staff Managers, the guys that get measured on doing timely appraisals. I had a big smile on my face when I said, "You guys have got to admit you have just about the best job in the world." They weren't smiling. They were deathly afraid that I was going to take their cakewalk job and turn it into something that required actual work. They were right.

"You get paid for on-time appraisals, which doesn't make any sense to me since that's your job. So, you'll keep doing that. In the meantime, our turnover rate is as bad as the rest of the industry right now. You need to cut that by two thirds." Everyone gasped because the turnover rate had been getting worse. I continued.

"I don't want to keep paying recruiters just to replace people. I want to add people to the billable ranks. So make sure the ones we have don't quit. We'll develop new targets in the morning. You will also have a new manager. No more paladins.

"If we increase volumes the way I'm planning, everyone in this room will make substantially more money. If our numbers don't change, most people here will make less money." I looked about the room. "Any questions?"

Silence.

I tried again. "You folks must have a question or two."

Silence

I turned to Betty Sue, who was leaning her face on one hand while drumming her fingers slowly on the table. "Come on, Betty Sue, you always have a comment or two." This, incidentally, was before the big expletive explosion scene with Belinda.

"Yeah, I've got a comment," she sneered. "People are going to *hate* you."

I moved over toward her and looked her right in the eyes. "Well, that's just fine with me because I'm not running for homecoming queen." I looked around the room and finished the discussion soberly. "And this is going to work." I left a stunned group of people.

This was the first time I had used the expression "running for homecoming queen." I kind of liked it.

We grew 74% the following year and virtually everyone made a lot more money.

(By the way, a couple of the sales people hated me, just as Betty Sue predicted. It was a power thing. They wanted the prestige of running a big operation combined with the pay they got without actually managing the operation. No way for me to win that one.)

There was one other trap I could have fallen into which came into vogue in the 90s. It was the consensus management trap. This essentially makes everyone part of the decision. And I don't mean the decision process; I mean the decision itself. I'm embarrassed to admit it but even IBM tried a flavor of this in the early 90s. I know. I had to attend one of the management re-training sessions. I rebelled.

Shortly after my 're-training", at IBM, I was notified by my boss that he was moving yet another organization under me, effective the following Monday. Getting a new boss is always a bit scary (I know I don't like it. It's like a stranger is taking over the tribe). To make them feel welcome, I scheduled a breakfast for the new group at the Four Seasons Hotel, just across from the IBM building.

The group had not had the success hoped for when they were first commissioned a year prior. They were a technical group run by an engineer who had received a battlefield promotion and who had not undergone the normal screening and then training an IBM manager gets. He was a bit of a group-think kind of guy because that's the way engineers solve problems on a big team.

I made the normal remarks welcoming them and then I talked about some plans for the future. And then for some reason I started thinking about that stupid, near-consensus class on Transformational Management that I had been sent to San Francisco to take. So I brought it up.

"As you know, many of us in management have been sent to the new classes that are aimed at more of a *'cooperative'* style of management." I looked around. A few people nodded in recognition. "And as you know, there is more of an emphasis on consensus, which I suppose I can understand." I looked around to a reasonably receptive group. I continued. "I can understand it, but I am not going to do it. You want input to a decision, then talk to me quickly. We need to get this ship turned around and it's not going to be done in a group hug. So please don't be offended when I don't ask you to vote. If a decision is mine to make, I owe it to you to make it. If it's your decision, you alone are responsible to make it and I expect more often than not you'll produce good results. So that's it. I'm a benign dictator. No consensus."

They cheered. Just like me, they were sick to death of no one taking responsibility. We felt then the same way a lot of women feel about men these days. Women want men to act like men. Show some guts. Employees want people in positions of leadership to lead. Show some guts.

Here's the rule:

Do not share the responsibility for a decision that is yours to make.

Get their input and make the decision. If you can't get their input, then make the decision anyway.

There is another version of this groovy-style management that popped up in the late 80s and early 90s. It was called matrix management. In companies like DEC, you had a lot of overlap of marketing and technical operations. This sometimes led to turf wars and sometimes it led to inaction. This was true at just about every computer technology firm out in the marketplace trying to sell things.

However, DEC (Digital Equipment Corporation), the original mini-computer powerhouse, had a solution. If you were in a group that had both technical and marketing folks, in fact if you were in any kind of organization with more than one operational discipline, you were managed via a matrix. You could have a boss that was an engineer on one side and then for certain other activities, the lead boss might be a sales guy or a program director. Thus, you had at least two bosses at any given time. It was hard being an employee with more than one boss. But think about being a manager when you really have not got the final authority.

These days when you go to DEC headquarters...

Wait! There is no DEC headquarters. They're gone! They fell flat so fast under matrix management that they had to sell themselves to Compaq, a maker of PCs, who in turn got gobbled up by HP. DEC, a great company, died under matrix management. Some people have said to me that they think a number of other things caused the downfall of DEC. The people who say this to me don't realize evidently that I wasn't asking for theories. I had friends at DEC. Everybody knows what happened to DEC. Whatever problems they had in the field, they were unable to solve quickly in a fast moving market due to matrix management.

Here's the rule:

If you have more than one manager, you have no management.

This also applies to project ownership, etc.:

If you have more than one owner, you have no ownership.

Here is as close as I will allow a manager to get to the above kind of stuff. It's called MBWA, otherwise known as Management By Walking Around.

In the morning, grab a couple of cups of coffee, go sit in a subordinate's office or by his or her desk, hand him a cup of coffee and ask what's going on. Chit chat a little and then move on. Do that every once in a while but be careful not to step on the toes of managers between you and their employees, especially if you still have the urge to run for homecoming queen now and then.

Many large companies have something like an annual opinion survey. IBM had one that typically had about 50 or 60 questions on it. Five of the questions were what they called the "Morale Index." I can't remember all of them but they were things like how you rate the company overall as a place to work, how you rate your boss, how you rate your pay, and so forth.

These surveys were potentially lethal for bad managers. If you weren't making your numbers <u>and</u> your people didn't like you, then you better have a real strong benefactor up the chain of command somewhere who is willing to use up one of his tickets for you.

The scoring for each question went:

> Very Satisfied
> Satisfied
> Neither Satisfied nor Dissatisfied
> Dissatisfied
> Very Dissatisfied

In terms of scoring, you might think that the middle category is a neutral but it's not. If your people answer a question about their "trust and confidence" in you and they check the "Neither Satisfied nor Dissatisfied" box, you get a negative. Typically, you need a minimum of about 59% positive to feel comfortable in your job.

When we reviewed it for my organization, there were some interesting results. First, my scores on the key assessments of me by my people were 88/11. Looking closer, 88% of the people were mostly very satisfied, and 11% wanted me dead. We could not figure out where the other 1% went. Another important stat was that my people gave survey scores to the managers above me that were much higher than those executives got elsewhere. That's because even if I completely disagreed with my bosses, I never let my people know that. Doing otherwise is called transparent management, which can destroy you.

Transparent management is another item in the toolkit of those running for homecoming queen. Instead of saying I'm not going to give you a raise, you say, "Sorry, Leslie, I'd like to give you a raise but my boss Fred just won't approve it." Even if that were true, you don't tell Leslie that. You say, "Leslie, you won't be getting a raise. Let's set some objectives for you that will make a raise possible on the next go around." Fred has nothing to do with it. As soon as it becomes clear that your boss Fred is making the decisions, people are going to look right past you and start trying to work with Fred directly. You become transparent to them. You lose any semblance of ultimate authority for your unit.

So don't run for homecoming queen and don't play the Fred-won't-let-me card.

In summary, if you're the captain, be the captain. If you spend a bunch of time below deck drinking grog with the crew, you may think that they think you're a swell guy. But what they're actually thinking is, "What are you doing down here? Who's running the ship?" After a while they'll ask you, "Don't you think you should be up there looking out for us, you know, watching for a storm or a big rock or something – maybe a little navigating with that sextant thingy?"

Be someone your employees can respect. If they like you as well as respect you, that's great but popularity is not the goal you pursue.

Side Note: You have often heard some manager say, "This is not a democracy; it's a business." That's true legally but one must understand that we Americans view life as a democracy. We think there should be democracy everywhere on earth. If we think North Korea should be a democracy, why wouldn't we naturally "feel" that GE or Prudential Insurance should be a democracy? Intellectually, we know better. However, we don't feel right when things look too dictatorial. As managers we don't want people to vote and we don't want to force a consensus. But we want to let people feel like they have some input along the way. MBWA is a good start. Just make sure you don't share the burden of management decisions. It's on your shoulders. And it comes back heavier every time you try to spread it around.

Chapter Four
Leadership Mistakes
(I'm an expert because I've done all of these)

The function of a manager is to have the right people doing the right things at the right time. In certain Hollywood movies and some corporate training films, this actually happens. In real life, you can get pretty close, but only for a while because the world changes and turns into a can of worms, yet you still have the same people you had when the world was perfect.

One of the "joys" of middle management is listening to a first line manager tell you what is wrong with all his employees. He does this for a reason. If he had perfect employees, then you might expect him to achieve his or her objectives. But since you purposely made those objectives a challenge, they are now sitting in your office complaining that they don't have the tools to get the job done.

Here is a summary conversation with all the managers who have told me how bad their employees are:

> First Line Mgr: Charles, you have given me sow's ears.
>
> Charles: So I shouldn't expect a silk purse, should I?
>
> First Line Mgr: That would be a stretch.
>
> Charles: I understand. Then all I want you to do is to make me a sow's ear purse that sells for as much as a silk purse. I really don't care how it gets made.

I really don't care because I have almost never seen a business unit comprised of people, all of whom were wrong for the job. So I know he doesn't have all sow's-ear employees. On the other hand, I have never known a perfect person, let alone a business unit full of them.

So, here is a sad fact of life:

Bad managers tend to focus on the weaknesses of their employees.

They believe if they can eliminate or minimize the weaknesses of their employees, all that will be left are the strengths. It's not only wrong; it's cruel. And here's the absurdity of it. It's as simple a paradox as occurs anywhere in nature. If the strengths are something you strive to isolate, then they must be worth something. If they are worth something, then put them to work and forget about the weaknesses. By the way, if you are focused on an employee's weakness, what do you think he or she is spending a lot of useless or negative time thinking about?

Here's the rule:

**Good management focuses on an employee's strengths
to direct them toward the needs of the business**

Unless someone's shortcomings and foibles are seriously hurting the company or the employee, don't spend a lot of time on them. Focus instead on what the employee can do to help you achieve your objectives.

What does this sound like in real life (well, sort of real)?

"Charles, this wrench you gave me is just terrible. Every time I go to pound a nail with it, the nail bends, flattens and becomes useless. And every time I use that hammer you gave me to remove hex nuts, the edges just round off!"

Most of my good employees have had weak spots, in some cases, glaring weak spots. My first job was to deploy them into tasks that utilized their strengths. If I did my job as a manager, the employee's weaknesses just became a source of entertainment between that employee and me over a couple of beers.

68

Anybody can gripe about their people. Capable managers will take these same imperfect people and achieve great results. My management team at STAR took the same group of people I inherited and went from almost no growth to 74% growth. I guarantee you they did not fix all their people's flaws.

Let's focus on some specific mistakes that managers make.

If the function of a manager is to have the right people doing the right things at the right time, then why would a manager try to undo his own work? It happens. Sometimes, it's called:

The Monkey on the Back Problem

Here's an example, one of a billion. This happens all the time.

Setting: Rachel is a top saleswoman in the telecom supply business. Fred, her boss, wants to see how she is doing in hitting her quarterly target. He asks her to stop by:

Fred:	So, Rachel, how are things looking for making your March 31st numbers?
Rachel:	It's going to be close.
Fred:	I thought you said it was in the bag. What happened? (Fred starts to sweat) I mean, I already told Charles that we're going to make the target.
Rachel:	I thought we could do it easily but deliveries on the 1031s are running behind.
Fred:	So, if I can get the factory to speed up the shipment of 1031s, you'll hit your March target?
Rachel:	You bet!

Fred picks up the phone and asks his secretary to get him the number of the factory that makes 1031s. Rachel mouths the words, "Thank you," as she walks off.

Every couple of days or so, Rachel wanders by Fred's office. She sips her coffee and asks, "So, Fred, how ya doin' on those 1031s?"

As March approaches, Fred runs to Charles, who happens to be Fred's boss. He taps nervously at Charles' door. Charles is generally pretty pleasant but he can also be a bit of an S.O.B. Fred has a gnawing feeling that this might be one of those times he gets to see the S.O.B. side of Charles.

> Fred: Charles, I need some help from you if you want me to hit my numbers.
>
> Charles: I'll come back to the last part of that statement later. First, what kind of help do you need?
>
> Fred: Well, Rachel's been selling up a storm but she doesn't see how she can make her quota for the 1st quarter if she can't get delivery on the 1031s.
>
> Charles: So, what's this got to do with me – or you for that matter?
>
> Fred: You see, I looked Rachel right in the eye and I asked her point blank, "If I can get you delivery on all of your 1031s, will you hit your numbers?" She had as much as said that already but I wanted to hear it again. *(Fred sounds a bit tougher than we recall, doesn't he?)*
>
> Charles: So, if *you* get her the deliveries, she'll make it. If *you* don't get the deliveries, she and therefore *you* won't make those quarterly numbers?
>
> Fred: Uh, well...
>
> Charles: So, if she makes her quota, does she get the bonus or do you?

Fred: Uh, well...you see... she had done everything she could to get the 1031s but the factory just wouldn't commit to a first quarter ship date.

Charles: Have you had any better luck?

Fred: No.

Charles: And now you're in my office trying to put the monkey on my back.

Fred: I guess I...

Charles: What you should have said is that you would make a call for her but if delivery remains constrained on 1031s, then she better find something else to sell that the factory *can* deliver. She needs to make her numbers - as do you - as do I.

Fred: So, now what do I tell her?

Charles: I don't know, Fred. But I'm telling you, you have a month to figure it out. And because I'm in a good mood today, might I suggest you tell her the same thing?

Fred: But she's been kind of depending on me to get those 1031s.

Charles: Did you tell her you make them in your garage?

Fred: No.

Charles: Then it sounds like she depended on the wrong guy for 1031 deliveries. The two of you have a month to figure out what to do. I'll make some calls for you but with a month left, don't count on anything big in the way of deliveries.

As Rachel stood sipping her coffee outside of Fred's door each morning, watching him dial for dollars, who was in the managerial role? Who was supervising whom?

Here's the rule:

Do not remove from the employee the ultimate burden of producing results.

If you want to help out, that's great. Just make sure the employee knows that even if you fail to provide adequate assistance, even if you said you could or would, the employee still must meet his or her objectives.

If you don't make this clear up front on something that looks like your action could be a key to success, then you are in the process of putting the monkey on your back. If you do what Fred did, you are essentially saying the employee does not have to perform until you do. As Charles, remarked, if she can't get deliveries on 1031s, then she needs to go sell something else.

Putting the monkey on your back is most often seen in younger, less experienced managers trying to prove that they are the driving force in the organization. They have confused leadership with being the star player. They are just looking for one of the employees to mess things up so they can step in and "show 'em how it's done." I've seen young managers, especially young men, walking around with several monkeys riding comfortably on their backs. In the case of some managers, there is a fear of not being valued and accepted. In the case of others, it is a desire to be a hero and a rock star.

There is another similar mistake managers make. It has to do with how they handle:

THE DUMPER.

Dumpers are guys that bring you their problems and expect you to solve them on the spot. Sometimes this is just out of habit and sometimes it's a ploy to be able to say later, "Hey, I told you there was a problem and you seemed to think it was no big deal." Or, "I brought you the problem and you didn't have any answers, either."

I had one particularly clever employee, John Baker that I inherited from a departing manager. He was what they called "too clever by half." I'm not sure what that means. I've only heard old people say it but everyone seems to know it means he was noticeably tricky, as in sneaky-tricky.

Here's one of our early conversations. John walks into my office uninvited, hands me a piece of paper and slumps in his chair across from me. I'm already pissed.

John: So, Charles, there's my summary of how this thing's heading at Acme Corp. They have been cutting back on expenses and I'm figuring we'll lose half our business there in the next 6 months. Yep.

I read the paper and then set it next to me. I didn't show any emotion.

Charles: Wow, John that looks like a tough one.

I then held my hand out, waiting for the next piece of paper, knowing that there wasn't one.

John (confused): What? What are you looking for?

I held my hand out a bit longer then pretended to realize my error.

Charles: Oh, I'm sorry. I must have the second page here and I didn't see it.

John: There's no second page.

Charles: Then did you write it on the back of this one? (I pick it up and look)

John:	Write what?
Charles:	*Your* recommendation for fixing this mess and what I can do in the way of resources, etc. to help you carry out *your* recommendation. Because if you don't have a recommendation then we are just conducting a half meeting here and I don't do half meetings. I mean, for heaven's sake, what do you want me to do with this piece of paper when I read it? Do you want me to feel bad? Do you want me to cry? Should I sell my stock? Tell me what to do, John.
John:	Well, I was hoping to …
Charles:	To dump it on me just like you used to do with Dave. The difference is that Dave came from the Office Products Division and always felt like he should have known more about large computers and you played on that guilt. Dave was a good guy and you ran him into the ground with this kind of crap. So here's what I need to see: A one-pager on what you plan to do to fix this and who at the client you plan to call on, who I need to call on and any resources you think will keep us from your dire prediction of a 50% reduction.

John got up to leave. The anger I was holding started to pass but not entirely. He had contributed greatly to the demise of Dave, a terrific guy who was just in over his head. But John probably had never intended for that to happen. This was just his way of doing business. I asked him to sit back down.

| Charles: | John, here's the thing. I'm not Dave and you need to quit trying to do what you did to him. No more games. Just lay it out for me and tell me what you're going to |

74

do. And do this every time a situation comes up – good or bad. I don't want any more surprises – good or bad. No more dumping problems on my lap and seeing if I can solve the puzzle in time. This is your puzzle. You solve it.

I have always been a roll-up-your-sleeves kind of manager, when necessary. With guys like John, you have to set the ground rules. Otherwise, they will abuse you. John got better at keeping me in the loop. He was actually very smart. When I got promoted to New York, he and I parted as good friends.

One other person that I inherited in the same office was a guy who liked to skate. He was always messing things up, mostly due to lack of effort, and then he would have great excuses. His prior boss commented on how hard it was to "pin him down."

Ed was the first person I ever forced out of the business. He began piling up the excuses for inaction and missteps. I all but begged him to just be honest with me but he always acted surprised and tried to make me feel like I was the one who was causing problems by asking him if he had kept his commitments.

I got a call one morning from the 4th floor receptionist. She told me there was a classroom full of people waiting for Ed. He was a half hour late for a class he had agreed to conduct for one of the accounts he was assigned to. We were trying to sell a company-wide office system (pre-Internet) and Ed felt the best way to do it was to get all the administrative managers at the customer account to buy in.

It was a good idea - except for the fact that he didn't show up to carry it out.

I called his home and got the classic, sleepy, "heh-hehlloooooo?" I apologized for waking him prior to noon on a Tuesday and then I told him about the class full of people. I heard a gasp and then he recovered quickly, singing, "Oh, that's not supposed to be todaaaay."

I explained that 30 people from several of the customer's various offices thought otherwise. He then blamed his secretary for not sending out the cancellation notice. I hung up and walked out to his secretary's desk and smiled at her as I waited for the phone to ring. It did. I asked if I could answer it for her. She looked perplexed as I reached for the phone. Ed sounded perplexed when he heard me say cheerfully, "Debbie's desk. May I help you?"

I explained to him that he would have to call back. I was here at Debbie's desk demanding an explanation for her failure to notify 30 people of Ed's sleep schedule.

Ed still didn't learn after that. So, I brought him in after another egregious act and went over a list which had exactly 14 items on it. It is wrong to save up all your gotcha stuff against an employee until his or her annual appraisal. This was more of a six-week horde. I had been hording because I was stumped. My boss kinda liked Ed, so I wasn't getting much help there.

True to form, he had an excuse for every infraction. I laid down my list and said, "Ed, I am 80% sure that your explanation is sort of adequate for all of these. There are 14 of them, if you were counting. However, I am also sure that 20% of what you are telling me is rubbish. So the math is .20 times 14 which still puts you about 3 in the hole."

He looked very confused at my math. I let him try to figure it out. "Ed, all I'm trying to do is give a bullshit response to your bullshit excuses. You're skating. Your history here is that you have always skated. You're not going to skate any more. Skating is the equivalent of lying. I'm done. You're done. Let's get together tomorrow morning and talk about what's next."

The next morning, I had set aside two hours to work out an Improvement Plan. This is a formal document; much like a performance plan but it has a short time limit on it. If the employee does not successfully meet the requirements, he or she is fired. My first act when Ed came in was to explain to him that he was being appraised a 5 under his old plan. A five means: "Did Not Meet the Requirements of the Job." There were four passing grades and one failing grade in the IBM system. Ed was about to receive the IBM version of an "F".

But it was not to be. Ed resigned. We worked out a severance arrangement and then I walked down to my boss's office and got him to sign off. Since firings and separations are a potential legal situation in the making, there must always be at least two levels of signoff. Beyond that, it ensures some degree of fairness for the employee in situations where the boss is potentially just "out to get" him or her.

My boss was delighted to see Ed leave. He had viewed Ed as a fun fellow but he couldn't stand him as a worker. When I asked him why he hadn't stepped up to this years ago, he said he could never quite "nail Ed down."

I went back to my office and talked to Ed while all the paperwork was being put together by HR. We had a great talk. He felt like I was doing him a big favor. He was another one of those people who came over from the Office Products Division in the merger of the divisions a couple years earlier. He felt like he never fit in and that's why he had started the skating. Like so many of the office product guys, he felt that you had to know the depths of computer technology to be able to sell big iron. We DP Division guys had made a lot of the office guys feel that way. It was wrong. This was also a failing of IBM executive management in terms of assimilating these people. I often wonder if it wasn't a purposeful failing. "Let's slap 'em all up against the wall and see who sticks!" is the expression, I believe. Most of them didn't stick. To me, it was tantamount to a layoff.

Ed and I talked about what he could do. I suggested that he should take on a single product or a piece of software, get to know it inside and out, and really drive it. He had already come to a similar conclusion. He left and I didn't hear from him again until one day I got a call at my Midtown Manhattan office. Ed wanted to take me to lunch and thank me. He had tracked me down after being one of the top salesmen that year for a little company in the word processing business. He made a couple million dollars selling software that finally put a bullet in his old product line, the typewriter.

Here's the rule:

When an employee is skating, *he* is on thin ice, not you.

You don't need to prove anything other than the fact that stuff just isn't getting done.

Skating is like the monkey-on-the-back challenge. In this case, the monkey is on your back to explain, figure out, or come to peace with the employee's behavior. To this I ask you just one question:

"Are you kidding me?"

SUBTLE DUMPING

The last of these, should have followed the situation with John, the dumper. [Please note: as a manager you should never label people i.e. dumper, skater, etc. As a writer, it feels really good].

In the case of subtle dumping, the employee puts you in a spot where you have to prove your case perfectly in order to gain his or her full buy-in or cooperation.

If after each attempt at explaining your position, the employee responds with a series of statements such as: "I'm not sure what you're asking me?" and then, "I'm still not quite getting how I fit into all this." And then "Maybe, I'm a little slow here but I'm still not sure what you're expecting from my involvement."

When I was a young manager, I had a visceral reaction to this situation. At about the point where I realized I was being toyed with by someone who was being purposely obtuse, I responded...how should we say it... colorfully. My choices of words were typically only heard when you dropped a shipping container on a longshoreman's foot. Such words were creatively used as syllable separators. Often, they were combined with a flagrant violation of the no-labeling rule and a great degree of political incorrectness, as I selected from a variety of terms for a mentally incapacitated person.

Now, as a more mature manager, I respond differently. I have added adverbs and gerunds to the parts of speech that are ...colorful.

The last time this happened was when I was doing a re-org that was badly needed in a company that was being merged into another company. Everything fit neatly into the new business strategy with the exception of one smaller organization, led by Vince, a person who was often condescending to everyone around him. When I called him and his new boss into my office to give them a preview, I was polite and upbeat. Vince was very circumspect and displayed a great deal of "patience" with me as I explained how I wanted him to take his organization forward. When I was done, he said, "I don't get it." I asked what part he didn't *get*. "I guess I don't know what you would call 'the greater organization.' I mean what is this...*thing*?" When he asked that question he did this set of hand gestures like he was making a loaf of bread out of mucous, hoping to form it into something that didn't look quite as awful as the recipe I was offering.

I pointed out that the mission was broader than the organization he was coming from but there were a lot of overlap and complementary skills, creating an opportunity for some new services and new revenue streams. (A little messy here, I admit).

He sat back in his chair and tossed his hands up in the air slightly. He said, with a smarmy little smile, "I...I'm just not seeing what you're thinking this will accomplish." He then turned to the person who was about to be his new boss and said, "Kyle, can you perhaps help me make a little better sense of all this?"

Kyle started to open his mouth to explain and I roared in, "I don't need an interpreter! Kyle is not here to sell you on this. *I* am not here to sell you on it, either. You now have ALLLLLLLLL the information I am ever going to give you on this subject. You are a smart guy; you have lots of smart guys working for you; you see what my broader mission is; it is now your job to take advantage of it and make this work, despite my pitiful attempt to impress you. This ain't paint-by-numbers' management, pal. Go figure it out."

He did.

There is almost no job, no assignment, no project that can be perfectly defined. Sometimes it gets kind of messy but you have a general idea of what is expected of you and what you can accomplish. Sometimes what you are setting out to do could be accomplished in a much better way than you designed it. This has happened to me more than once. With the exception of Vince, I could sit down with the person and get there via successive approximations. Every once in a while, I would see that what I was asking them to do was not quite right. I would then either revise it or undo my initiative altogether. With guys like Vince, you are forced to field-test it with live ammo. He wouldn't cooperate and have a working session with us on it. It's bad management. It's bad business.

Here's the rule:

You do not have to prove to the employee that your decisions and directives are worthy.

Accepting healthy challenges from an employee is part of your job. If Vince had felt that there was significant danger to the company, the client, or his people, I would have listened. All he needed to do was seek some latitude in implementing it and perhaps a little bit of time beyond what would normally be expected. He could then come back to me and say, "Here's my plan. Is this what you were thinking?" Instead, at my insistence, he got to come back and make a presentation, proving *he* had figured it out. That's not good. Because now that he knows I'm really irritated with him, he's going to tell me mostly what I want to hear – recycling my own words. That is not a constructive management dialog.

The mistake was partly mine. I knew Vince could be like that. I could have started the conversation by telling him this was a bit of a brainteaser and then enlisted his help in figuring it out. Still, whether I started the conversation that way or not, I couldn't let Vince put me in a position where I had to give him a watertight job description before I could expect anything at all from him – like cooperation.

Chapter Five

Recognition

Public Awards and Other Man-Made Disasters

There are three basic utility functions required of management: Communication, Delegation, and Recognition.

I wrote the rough draft of this chapter, longhand on a lined pad with a #2 pencil during an out of town trip I took recently. When I got back and reread the sections on communication and delegation, I said to myself, "This is really boring. There is no way I'm going to re-key all that into the computer." So, if you're really curious, call me and I'll fax you my notes.

Both communication and delegation are predicated on just one simple issue: how you view your role? What is your job? Are you the guy that creates the problem and then works with your people to see things through to success or are you the hero who lays out the agenda and then proceeds to supervise every aspect of your people's performance?

Do you know what you want? Can you create a few critical measurements and wait for the report or do you have to touch everything constantly until you "feel" like it's all heading in the right direction?

Can you communicate what you want and then follow up or do you have to walk out of the office and follow your employee around while he or she does the job?

Is your communication two-way? Do you actually listen or are you just waiting for the employee to stop talking so you can make your brilliant remark – and regain control?

Can you reduce the usage of the word "I" to a minimum?

Okay, now go practice for a few years and then come back and we'll talk about moving you into upper management.

As I said, that's kind of boring, academic stuff and I just can't get into it. That's why God sprinkled a few professors onto the planet. If you actually have to live and breathe communication and delegation, you know it's a hairball. You don't want to write about it. But as a professor, it's a very clean and logical subject. So go read a book by a professor and then come back to the real world and get your brains beat out. I do however, cover it extensively in classes I teach. In a class I can be clever and fun, even on communication and delegation

RECOGNITION

Recognition, on the other hand is an interesting topic because the people doing the recognizing often forget that the process inevitably involves Earthlings.

This is stunning because the people doing the recognizing are often themselves Earthlings. They should know that outside of the need for security, the single biggest craving of all human beings is the desire to be appreciated.[4]

It is an ongoing desire. It's just like breathing. Yet we treat it as something you do every once in a while at a branch meeting or the annual kickoff.

Here's the rule:

Recognition is something you do all day and every day.

---

[4] Maslow puts self-actualization at the top of his famous hierarchy of human needs. It's beyond the point where you *need* the approval of others to drive your actions. However, there is still a fine line between *want* and *need* and the actions they produce. I don't know anyone who doesn't want a little approval from his or her fellow human beings. There are people who *act* like they don't care what others think. They are called...let's see, it starts with the letter...

The only exception to this rule is when there are no other humans involved. Pipefitters, for example, can often go the whole day without recognizing or appreciating other people because they are down there alone - with pipes.

We'll come back to this concept (ongoing recognition - not pipefitting) at the end of this section. For now, we need to look at acts of special recognition, such as awards. Let me make it clear, this section is about the subject of recognizing excellence in performance; in other words, recognition of specific achievements. It can range anywhere from saying, "Good job!" to sending someone to Hawaii for two weeks for closing some huge deal.

But first, let's dispel a few misconceptions.

Myth #1

Paying someone really well is the same as recognition.

Have you heard the tough-guy bosses who say, "I don't need to tell him, 'Good job.' I *pay* him to do a good job."

This is right from the handbook of Jerk Management. Even as CEO, I wanted an attaboy now and then. Even those of us who are completely self-actualized get a little more peppy when someone tells us that something we did or said was good.

When the above practitioner of Jerk Management makes his imperious remark, keep in mind, he's doing it to impress you. He wants you to think he's cool and above all of this stuff. He wants you to admire him. He wants to be recognized. He is, in other words, a steaming column of... hypocrisy.

Myth #2

Public recognition is better than private recognition.

One old school manager once said to me, "If you can't do recognition in public, then maybe it's an indication that the recognition itself is not quite right." I couldn't disagree more.

Special recognition - bonuses, trophies, awards, etc. have two elements: the actual reward of cash, trips, trophies and the act of conveying appreciation. For the latter, what kind of setting gives you the ability to convey the personal sentiment of appreciation better? I personally loathe public recognition events. It has been said that when you recognize one guy in of a group of 15 people, you have essentially de-recognized the other 14. There's a lot of truth in that.

I'm not one of these people who say everyone's a winner. The self-esteem movement in our education system is a joke. Thirty kids compete and everyone gets a trophy? That had to have been dreamt up by some real loser who finally found a way to make sure no one was ever a real winner again.

I ran varsity track. I almost always won. The two times I came in second still haunt me. The time I lost to Mikelson in the 800 was especially disturbing. My times that season were better than his; so when I headed into the straightaway, I was well in front and I kept it steady, knowing I had to run the first leg of the 4 x 400 which started less than twenty minutes after the completion of the 800.

When I looked up at the stands to see the sweet gal who kept our team records, she had a look of angst on her face which was quickly blocked out by Mikelson stepping in front of me at the finish line. If someone had tried to hand me a little trophy saying, "You're a winner too, Charles," I would have kneed him in the groin. I lost. I was an idiot. I was thinking about the next race when I should have been winning the race I was in. Mikelson came from behind like…what's the word?......... a winner! There was *one* first place guy.

86

The difference between a track meet and a business environment is considerable. You can make a few parallels but they wear thin when you look a little deeper. In the race with Mikelson, we started at exactly the same time and we had exactly 800 meters to go, once the gun went off. He and I were running against the same four other guys. The weather was the same in my lane as it was in Mikelson's. I wish someone would come up to me some day and tell me a secret about Mikelson's steroid use or how the night before the meet, they were secretly able to shave two meters out of Mikelson's lane. But the truth is I lost fair and square.

Almost nobody has it the same as the other guy in business. This doesn't mean everyone would do the same under the same circumstances. But when it comes time to make awards, people are very quick to rationalize how much tougher it was for them than the guy up at the podium. That's how we manage our self-esteem.

Even if people can come to grips that the other guy just did a great job, they're still not happy. They aren't motivated. They don't walk out of the award meeting saying, "Next year, that's going to be me up there!" Only in the movies and in the fantasy of some guy who has been in management too long does an award ceremony ever make someone recommit themselves.

Does anyone feel better when Fred walks up to the front of the room and gets a check for $5000? Not me. I'm covetous as hell. For a moment, I hope he gets rolled in the back alley and they take his watch too. People may act like good sports and congratulate Fred but they aren't happy. Just watch how many people go home early that day. Wait a few days so that people don't get accused of sour grapes and then listen to the Fred stories. They won't be hero-worshiping stories.

My fellow Earthlings, we got kicked out of the Garden of Eden because we are rotten creatures. Even when we have paradise, we want more. If it hadn't been the forbidden fruit it would have been something else. And ever since we left, our treatment of one another hasn't been exactly savory. I would have kicked us out even before the fruit stealing. I *know* us.

There have only been a couple of times in my entire career where handing out an award to one person felt good to me. I was a young trainee at IBM when Lee Carlisle got the award for winning back the Seattle First National Bank account from Honeywell. It was a huge victory. He had starved year after year, not making quota until finally he got the mulit-multi-million dollar order. We all cheered. The whole SeaFirst team got bonuses. Lee Carlisle cried real tears as he thanked everyone on the team and all the other people in the branch who helped him. Everyone got recognized who had taken a key role. (I think they did. How do I know; come to think of it.)

That victory deserved a huge party. Many don't.

My preference is to invite someone into my office and tell them how important or impactful something they did has been to the company. Then I give them the award and we talk about it. True, the meeting details eventually get out but at least you're not making people sit for an hour and swim impatiently in someone else's glory.

TYPES OF RECOGNITION

One of the awards I hand out for moments of glory is a night-on-the-town award for the person and his or her spouse. I tell them to go to dinner and a movie or a play, etc. and the evening is on me. Give them an expense limit of course, usually two or three hundred dollars, but remind them that their job is to hit that limit or more. If you just hand them the money, it isn't the same.

I was once picked as Manager of the Quarter for IBM's West Coast operations, headquartered in San Francisco. My wife and I were flown back to New York to stay at the Trump Plaza Hotel for a few days. We were allowed to pick some great Broadway plays to go see and we went to several wonderful restaurants. The whole thing probably cost IBM three thousand dollars. They could have given me the three grand and I would have squirreled it away. No memories. But I remember Lee Bowman giving me the award and saying that when he had narrowed the candidates down and he started asking for the opinions of some of the field executives, the consistent feedback was that I always delivered more than what was expected.

I remember his bluish tie. I remember exactly where he was standing when we shook hands. I remember it because that type of award made it memorable. So the advice is to give memories, if at all possible. Make creative trophies or plaques. I still have the ones that my employees at IBM gave me as a going away present. That was a long time ago. Here's another memory:

During a tough time in IBM's history, a bunch of us were sent to Squaw Valley California as a result of being nominated for and winning a creativity award. They took us on a hot air balloon ride – my first and only time. It was wonderful. I rode a mountain bike for the first time. I went for a 14 mile run in the mountains. I caught a hummingbird moth and then let it go. It looked just like a hummingbird. Do a Google image search. I caught one of those!

The point is, I remember and I have great feelings about the company from those times.

Some of the best awards I have given out have been from some of my crazy contests. They have been great for morale and I always make sure I get to participate in the prize.

It all started out innocently enough one time. Richard Rogers had an M&M machine on his desk and I love chocolate. When you pulled the M&M guy's arm, it dispensed a handful of candy. I drained it in a very short period of time and then I told Richard to refill it and expense the M&Ms as "office supplies." Soon, others wanted to provide "office supplies."

This worked out fine. The desktops were soon flowing with chocolate. But one day, I walked past someone's desk who had a jar of little Tootsie Rolls. Tootsie Rolls? Tootsie Rolls are *not* chocolate. They are cocoa-flavored vinyl. The person was chastised.

Then an even greater offense occurred. One of the employees on the other side of the office brought in a five pound jar of gumdrops. And they weren't even regular gumdrops; they were *spice* gum drops – cinnamon, cloves, spearmint, wintergreen, and …… something white. I was pretty bugged, as I walked away with my handful of gumdrops.

When I got back to my office, I set aside the white ones and then tried to figure out what flavor they were. I couldn't quite put my finger on it and the more I tried, the less I could distinguish the taste. I asked a couple of other people to try. They couldn't figure it out either.

So I created a contest.

The person who could correctly guess the flavor of the white gumdrops got to take me to the Dilettante Chocolate shop for dessert. They had amazingly decadent desserts and I couldn't wait for someone to win.

At the end of the first day, Brian, the person who had brought in the 5 pound jar of gumdrops, came to my office and explained that he had run out of gumdrops. It turned out that the whole building wanted in on the contest. There were approximately 18 floors of IBMers in that building. When they came to take samples of the white gumdrops, they helped themselves to the colored ones as well.

Brian went through several refills of "office supplies." He raised some concern about the fact that I had not put an end date on the contest. Finally, I agreed that the following Friday at 1 PM, the winner would be announced. I had several hundred entries. I had failed to state that each person could only make one guess. It was a poorly defined contest. There were several lunches awarded along the way for creative answers. The guy who guessed *mulberry* got to take me to the Four Seasons for lunch.

I came to my office a little before 1 PM that last Friday and my door was literally covered in signed sticky notes. There was only one problem.

I had no idea what flavor the white ones were.

So I picked the five flavors that sort of made sense, figured out who had submitted them first and then sent out a memo declaring the finalists. People were then permitted one vote, via email. The vote would be held the following Wednesday. This allowed for only two days of campaigning, which was extremely vigorous. Two of the people honestly thought they had the right answer. I had my secretary contact the makers of the gumdrops. She simply could not find anyone to tell her.

Of the hundreds of ballots cast, the overwhelming vote was for vanilla. I'll say it again: vanilla. There is no way I would let vanilla win. I'll say it again and you say it with me: vanilla.

I can't even remember what won. But for a few weeks, it was a lot of fun for everyone. These were tough times during IBM's transition but it wasn't the reason for the contest. It just seemed liked something fun to do. I had been caught in a regime change and had been given a group of only 4 people with which to rebuild an empire. Six months later there were 52 of us as a result of purely organic growth in a new area of business that had failed everywhere else in the country. Six months after that, all of consulting was part of the organization and everyone wanted to work in our operation. We were all building it together and respect for one another was high. We had a few former Andersen Consulting snots in our midst that made politics a bit unpleasant at times, but everything felt alive in a company that otherwise seemed like it was really struggling.

I had contests where the whole organization won if we made our targets. We went to the Mariners game and used the presidential suite. For another contest we went river rafting on the Wenatchee. For a big software contest, we went salmon fishing at Westport. People still talk about those contests.

In the meantime, lots of people were brought into my office, given awards, bonuses and promotions and nobody felt like something unseemly was taking place.

PROMOTIONS

This is a form of recognition that is usually misunderstood by people who want to move up in the company. Too often, someone does a stellar job and then feels they ought to be put into management or moved into middle or executive management.

Management and executive jobs are just that – jobs. I don't add receptionists just for fun and I don't add management positions just for fun. If the company is growing and expanding or if the company is creating new departments, then new management opportunities arise. However, if the company is more or less growing at a slow rate, then the career opportunities become less and you either have to be creative or you have to wait until someone vacates a management position for one reason or another.

When someone has done a great job for an extended period of time, I will often get a short visit by the person saying, "Charles, I would like to set up a meeting with you to talk about my career." Or I'll get a call from a subordinate manager saying, "Angie has done a great job, I'd like to come talk to you about moving her into management."

Here's the rule:

Create the job and *then* look for a candidate.

You should be identifying people as management potential candidates on an on-going basis. Most big companies have a war room in which are posted the key executive positions and by each position is a list of people who could fill that job. That way there isn't a mad scramble for candidates when a job suddenly comes open.

An executive in a fairly large company, which wasn't very professionally run, once brought me into his office to review a planned reorganization. He had been given a new assignment and was to take his entire division in a new direction. He showed me the org chart and the names of the people to fill it. They were all the same people now doing very different jobs.

I said, "Wow, Dave. I would call that a miraculous coincidence. Of the 6 billion people on Earth that could possibly fill those jobs, you just happen to have all of them already working for you."

It's important to promote from within but you have to be careful not to create a junta, where the same guys are always in charge, regardless of the skill set required. Be sure each time an opening comes up that the best person for the job goes into it.

When someone tells me how great they've done and therefore they should be made a manager, I have to help them understand how it works. I often use an illustration about why I believe I should be allowed to play for the Lakers. I'm smart and presentable and decent and I can pass behind my back. But at some point, someone may ask what I have done to indicate that I am ready to play pro basketball.

At some point, the person asking to go into management has to have shown some aptitude for directing the activities of others. Being a really good salesperson is important. But the fact that someone is great at sales does not mean they are great at sales *leadership*. In fact, a lot of people who are good at sales are absolutely not people you would want with authority over others. Let's face it, some salespeople are manipulators. Do you really want a manipulator managing your sales unit? A persuader is one thing. A manipulator is either lazy or does not believe in himself or herself. They don't think they can just lay it out there and say, 'This is what needs to be done and I want you to do it."

Here's another problem with people like that, I won't have them reporting to me. Yuk.

Promotion is a powerful form of recognition but it has to be a match between a bona fide opening and a qualified candidate. It is not to be considered as simply one of the many ways to recognize people because it is too important to the future of the business to try to match organizational changes to someone's latest performance victory.

RECOGNITION IN GENERAL

It's really pretty simple. Make people feel like they are secure and valued on an ongoing basis. Smile. Ask them their opinion about things. Overlook their infrequent mistakes. Talk to them like adults. Disagree with them without making them feel like they've just tangled inappropriately with one of the gods. Send a person home when you find out one of his or her kids is sick and they are really having a hard time getting someone to look after the child. You're recognizing that parenthood is above the needs of the company.

I once did this. I overheard a woman on the phone trying desperately to arrange for someone to babysit her child. Her little girl was 4 and she was too sick for daycare. So I waited for her to get off the phone and I told her to go take care of her daughter. She felt guilty. She felt like that might hurt her job standing. I tried to persuade her otherwise. She finally agreed to go home. Twenty minutes later I came by and she was still on the phone. I walked over and whispered, "Don't mind me." I then opened her top drawer and slid a bunch of her papers into it. I then whispered, "Tell them you have to go." As she hung up her phone, I put her purse on her lap and wheeled her in her office chair out to the elevator. As she got on the elevator I whispered, "There, I feel better already."

Do the very hard job of putting pressure on people to perform without making them feel like they are in a pressure cooker. This is a way of recognizing that they are fellow human beings who, just like you, are struggling to get through every day. We're all struggling. Let's not make it harder on one another.

Speaking of which, let's talk about how we criticize one another – "constructively," of course.

Mini-Departure
To Critique or Not

Every mature person knows that criticism is a necessary part of life and that when it is leveled at him, he is potentially benefiting from it and therefore he should not bristle when being criticized.

So feel free to label me as *immature*, because I ___ hate it. I may smile and nod but at least momentarily, I am already plotting to get you back, someday, someway. I bristle. Taxonomically speaking, I am a member of a species beyond a wild boar in terms of bristly. Even friendly criticism causes my eyes to narrow just a bit. Do I feel abnormal saying this? Well, when it comes to criticism, I believe there are two kinds of people:

> Category 1: Immature people like me who will admit to the fact that we *hate* being criticized and...
>
> Category 2: Liars

Even when people say, "Charles, let me play devil's advocate..." I bristle. I don't want a devil's advocate unless I ask for one; which I only do when I am really wandering on some issue.

So, now that I have 98% of normal people on my side and perhaps a handful of the Category-2 types, let's talk about how to offer a critique that won't be viewed so negatively.

By the way, have you ever worked with (or for) someone who has a little tweak of refinement for everything you think, do or say? Please write to me with your revenge fantasy. I know you have one – and I'm collecting them.

I won't spend a lot of time on this; but remember: almost everything someone brings in to show you and get your opinion on is part of them. It's personal.

So, follow these rules and you'll be okay.

1. **Thank them for their effort, even if it's weak.**
2. **Start with the big stuff and then go to the small stuff.**
3. **Start with the good and then go to the "needs work" components.**

Understand *what* they were looking to achieve in the areas that are questionable. It might make sense. Even if it's ultimately decided to take it out of a proposal or other piece of work, at least you were thoughtful about it.

When nerds started to come into prominence and prestige in the 90s, due to their coding and development skills, things changed. Prior to that, engineers and other technical people were your soft- spoken, Type-B personality, steady-as-a-rock kind of people. They were pleasant.

When the nerds got going, they now had their chance to show they had value after 12 years of being dumped on or ignored in school. They developed hierarchies and power kluges. To show how much they knew, they savagely tore down anything else that someone did if they could find the least little flaw. That made them the nerd with the highest technical standards and expertise. If they were to miss ripping something apart and it showed up later with a flaw, it would hurt their standing with the other nerds.

That approach permeates whole companies now. Many geeks I know are socially horrible people. You can't show them anything without them attacking first and then reluctantly coming around to see some value. It is very destructive and it often limits what people will bring forward in the way of work and new ideas.

Don't do it. And don't allow it.

I had a business partner who couldn't learn that. People would come to his office and say they just put five people on a new project at the phone company, and he would say, with a sneer, "Well, that's good because last week, four came off one of your other projects. You're only one ahead for the whole month!"

Tell me what was gained by that kind of behavior. That was not the time to critique. There should have been two conversations. Congratulations on the sale. And then a couple days later, a review of the month's progress.

Be positive without being phony. This even has a code name: civility. We've spent the last 10,000 years learning how to "get to the bottom line" without always "cutting to the chase" in a nasty way. That way we don't have to keep burning down each other's hut. Civility works - and it reduces our carbon footprint.

Side note to Mini-Departure
Critiquing in the Millennial Age

It has always been true but now you can't even fake it. With Millennials you better not criticize unless you know...

The Rule

You have to earn the right to criticize, even if you're the boss.

If they don't know you care and that you are acting in their best interest, Millennials really don't care what you think. They will view it as an attack from someone who just doesn't get it. So, long before you get to the point of criticizing, establish a collegial relationship.

Chapter Six
Managers Behaving Badly

Management behaviors that lead to problems tend to stem from one of two sources:

- Fear of the employees
- Contempt for the employees

Most of the behaviors I have listed previously fall into the former category. The manager feels that he or she needs to be loved and admired to be able to continue to exercise authority. This explains the homecoming queen, monkey-on-the-back, acceptance of dumped problems. We as managers don't want to offend or appear unsupportive, so we do stupid things and mislead our employees as to what to expect from management. Then, when a new exec shows up and he's more like me, it gets kind of uncomfortable for a while – and sometimes downright nasty. In the meantime, before the management relationship gets fixed, either by me or by the subordinate manager figuring it out, there is a sub-optimization of productivity, to say the least.

The second set of behaviors is often seen in people who view other people as nothing more than a means to an end. This is often seen in younger managers who are on their way up the ladder, forced temporarily to spend time with "the little people."

Let's start with one that looks like a contempt issue but is really a fear issue.

THE GROUP BEATER

In every unit, there is at least one employee who does something that bugs you. It may be a pet peeve such as an annoying, unprofessional laugh; or a common peeve such as clipping nails during a branch meeting; or an actual problem such as rarely turning in required paperwork.

The manager should go to that person, explain that the behavior is not right and then come to an understanding that the behavior will be extinguished. Instead, what the group beater does is send out an email or stand up in a meeting and point out that employees cannot do this or that particular thing.

This behavior can be rationalized in many ways but here is the primary argument:

> *I hate to pound on an employee for something minor. I like to pick my battles. If I pull an employee into a meeting to tell him that I don't like such and such behavior, then that's the communication he carries around with him. That's what he thinks I'm focused on. Gosh, Charles that's kind of the opposite of what you said the other day when you said don't bug Generation X about the little stuff.*

My response:

"Are you saying that it's too small to bug one of your employees about it, but it's not too small to bug <u>all</u> of your employees about it?"

If it's too small to bug your employee about it, then don't bug your employee about it. If it's something that needs to be dealt with, have a quick, sterile discussion, put it in perspective and then move on. Just don't mix it into a meeting with something that actually *is* important.

All that is accomplished by group-beating is negative stuff. You're reminding everyone of what a grind it is at the factory. And for your target, the one or two guys you hoped would "get it," you have just told them that everyone else is doing it too.

Here's the rule:

On performance or behavioral issues, the only forum is one-on-one.

No public appraisals, good or bad. If you have an issue with any other human being, do it in private, just you and the other person. That way no one (including you) gets hurt or embarrassed.

Is this not Golden Rule 101 stuff?

INSIDER TRADING

In order to show his employees that he is "one of them" in spirit, a manager will often deal in information that was intended primarily for management. Whereas management all too often plays the game of kids and adults when it comes to information and decisions, there are those who go the other way and act as if *everything* should be public knowledge.

The truth is, certain facts and pieces of information, taken out of context or set forth at the wrong time can cause a lot of problems. In addition, inside traders often like to deal in gossip, which hurts other people. They will talk about someone who is not liked, because this shows that they are in with the generally good group of people who don't like *that* person.

When George Washington was 16, he wrote a book called *Rules of Civility & Decent Behavior In Company and Conversation*. I highly recommend the book. It's a short read, listing 110 social rules you should follow, almost all of which still apply. So go read it.

Here's George Washington's Rule #89:

Speak not Evil of the absent for it is unjust.

Get out of the habit of talking poorly about others, even when talking to your spouse or friends. It will have an amazing effect on your outlook and a transforming effect on your image with others. As juicy as it is to backbite, the people you are talking to always walk away wondering what you say about *them* when they are not around.

And get good at politely turning aside such discussion when someone else starts in. Every once in a while, you and other managers have to discuss an employee's bad behavior. That's part of management. Just don't turn it into a form of entertainment or some untoward catharsis.

Employees actually do not appreciate being let in on information that wasn't meant for them. They know indiscretion when they see it. They expect a manager to be more professional. Leaking shows bad judgment. They ask subconsciously, "Where else is he showing bad judgment?" They also ask themselves whether the indiscrete manager also shares some of the private conversations *they* have had with him.

And it buys you nothing other than a fleeting titillation response from the employee. Cheap thrills.

Here's the rule:

Never use business information as social currency.

Here's another rule:

People do not trust a man who betrays a confidence – including a confidence that is implied.

If your people can't trust you on the small things, how are they supposed to trust you with major decisions of business and personnel management?

MR. MOODY

Does the boss's response to a request depend on his mood? If it does, then doesn't the boss become the primary business concern and not the client or the competitor or all the other things an employee should be focused on?

Being moody, especially angry moody, is cruel. It makes it hard for your employees to get up each morning and come to work. It's like punching people except it isn't against the law. However, the fact that it hurts others doesn't seem to cut any ice with bad-ass managers. They toss out those remarks mentioned earlier like, "I don't get ulcers, I *give* ulcers!" What an ass.

Then let me make a case to the bad-asses out there, who want to survive. This case applies to managers, military officers, Presidents, the Fuehrer, doctors (the ones who make you feel stupid for asking questions), teachers, scout leaders and everyone who is vested with some degree of power over others.

Here's the rule:

If people fear you long enough, they will come to hate you.

Still, I know I'm not cutting any ice with certain managers. I once sat in a room with my boss and one of his moody peers. My boss pointed out to him that something Mr. Moody had done was going to make a lot of people unhappy or angry. Mr. Moody responded, "So? I'm not looking for any new friends." This is a lot different than running for homecoming queen. This is running for homecoming schmuck. That contest you *will* win, just by entering.

Moody bosses kill morale. Moody bosses stifle information flow. People measure their words or they wait until "just the right moment to broach the subject."

Who has time for that? I have had Moody bosses and I simply avoided them. I have no respect for them. I assume they act rotten because they aren't any good at what they do. The sick part is watching other people, fearful for their jobs or their careers, sucking up to the beast. I don't. I won't. And at times it has cost me. I'm okay with that too. Most of your people with any punch won't respect a person who can't or won't modulate his or her moods.

Thanks to Generation X, moody bosses are becoming rarer because it's just not having the same impact as it used to. Due to having indulgent parents that were trying to give us "the things they never had" because of the Depression, we baby boomers got the impression that it really *is* all about us. As a result, we care mostly about ourselves. That's why we're called the "Me Generation." But Gen-X types aren't exactly that way. The best way to put it is that they just don't care about *you*. In fact, they don't care about a lot of stuff and one of the things they don't care about is whether you're sitting in your office, smoldering with suppressed rage. If you have a nasty on, or a rock in your shoe or big stick up your butt, then it sounds like *you* have a problem.

It always pays to be positive. As a manager it's really not a matter of choice.

Here's the rule:

As a manager, you can be positive or you can stay home.

I said earlier that managerial moodiness isn't against the law. But it *is* against the rules. Many large companies actually put into the performance plan of managers something similar to what was in every IBM manager's performance plan: "You will be upbeat at all times." If you could not do this, you would eventually be taken out of management.

Also be careful about being tense, overly focused, aloof, distracted, habitually introspective, etc. These are close enough to mood issues that you will risk being something people have to deal with rather than someone they can work with.

Here's the rule:

It ain't about you.

So don't make it about you.
Which brings us to…

THE CLAIM JUMPER

I think I have a lot of novel ideas that I have come up with since I have had **MY** debut here as your manager. And I have a lot that I…

After you roll out the third "I" people start rolling *their* eyes.

We all know this kind of person. They are so focused on what everyone thinks about them or, more correctly, what they want everyone to think about them, that they start to fidget if the conversation moves to any subject where they can't demonstrate that they are smart, brave, or important. If you look outside and see a beautiful sunrise, they will agonize over how to take credit for it. Failing that, they will try to come up with a situation they were in so they can say that they have experienced a better or more meaningful sunrise, or a sunrise that brings back a memory of some heroic adventure.

As a manager, you can't do this. In fact, you have to go the opposite way. Unless you're writing your memoirs, you have to swallow your "I's" and "me's" and "my's" in favor of the employee. That doesn't mean you give credit where it isn't due. Never do that because it hurts your credibility and makes recognition less meaningful and therefore less effective. What it means is that you give credit to your employee and leave yourself out of it.

Here's the rule:

Do not focus on your part in the success of your employees.

When you focus on your contribution at the expense of the employee, it stifles employee initiative and hurts morale.

Claim Jumpers ooze insecurity through every pore. Some may argue that they are so focused on their career that Claim Jumpers steal credit merely to get ahead. My counter to that argument is that Claim Jumpers are so insecure, they can't trust their ability to get ahead based on their own business acumen.

A hybrid form of Claim Jumping is to give credit to the employee in person or in public and then when the manager gets with his or her own boss, they play down the employee's role and make it clear that the mouth-breathing employee could never have groped their way out of their mess had the hero manager not emerged from the phone booth in full cape and leotards.

If you don't think that sits poorly with an executive, then you have completed the third point on the Claim Jumper triangle: Fool your employees, fool your boss and fool yourself. The problem with that triangle is there is really only one side. You have fooled yourself into thinking you have fooled the employees and your boss.

Managers also have to watch out for employees who claim-jump. Unless you protect the integrity of the merit system, you will hurt initiative and create a system that favors lying.

If you have someone who is a Claim Jumper, point it out to him – the sooner the better:

Charles: When you talk about something that you and other people have been working on, it often sounds like you were the central character and the rest were walk-ons and factotums. That hurts everyone and causes distrust.

Fred: That wasn't my intent.

Charles: Good. Then don't do it.

With a manager, you might want to be a little more heavy-handed. You need to remind him or her that the job of a manager is to help develop the strengths of the employee. Tell the manager that he or she will be measured on business unit results *and* growth of the employees in the unit. The manager needs to understand that the higher he or she goes in the corporation, the more critical it is to lever the strengths of the people below them in the organization. If managers have more personal success stories or show that they are the real heroes, then they have failed in one of two ways functionally: they don't have the right people working for them or they have not put those people in situations where they will do great things. If they have great people but are still focused on themselves, then they have yet another failing as a manager: recognition of good performance by the employee. This is one of the biggest destroyers of morale.

Earthlings have tribal instincts. We hate doing things and then not getting a pat on the back, peer recognition and/or approval from the chief.

Claim Jumpers hurt the whole village.

DEALING WITH TROUBLING PERSONNEL SITUATIONS

This is a politically correct way of saying here's what you do with pain-in-the-butt employees, but I can't refer to people as pains in the butt because my editor drives a Prius, wears Birkenstocks, and is easily offended.

If you think you have an employee who is a serious problem, then you have an employee who is a serious problem. And by the way, everyone else knows it too. The question everyone is asking, including the problem employee, is whether you will step up to it.

Remember this quote from Proverbs: *Even a child is known by his actions, by whether his conduct is pure and right.*

In other words: Nobody ain't foolin' nobody.

But not all troubling personnel situations are due to people who are doing evil. Sometimes, just plain rotten situations occur and they involve people who are solid citizens and who are making their performance targets. You still have to deal with it.

This is now HOW territory. How I suggest you handle the next set of employees, will give much broader insights than just for the problem at hand. So, to help you, I will give you the situation and then I will handle it the way most people who are untrained often handle it in one of my classes. By the way, these are for the most part real situations from my past and some of the mistakes that students make are exactly the mistakes I made in real life.

Let's start with a real watershed situation. This really isn't so much about a person hurting the whole village. It is designed to bring out techniques for dealing with an employee in a troubling situation:

AGATHA, THE STINKY EMPLOYEE

Even in role play, people are very uncomfortable with this one. So here is the setting: I put a situation description on the projector for all students to read. They get one minute and then I pick a person to be the manager. At that point, Agatha enters the room. I have had a number of people assist me in my classes but the best one for the role of Agatha was Heidi Sutton, who was the Director of the education division at a company where I was the CEO. As Agatha, she would come into the room, pull up a chair opposite the table where the student manager was seated and with a big smile, she would flap her coat to cool herself and the call would begin. Here's the situation as the students read it:

Agatha has a problem. You just received a phone call from the client saying Agatha has terrible body odor and she is destroying the productivity and morale of the project team. He feels we should deal with our employee in resolving the issue.

This isn't the first time you have heard this. Three weeks ago, a couple of your other employees complained about Agatha's odoriferousness. You now know she smells bad. You have asked her to come see you. She is wafting to your office at this very moment.

To set the scene in a little more detail, I always seated my students at tables connected together in a big U. We problem employees, Heidi and I, would enter the room and sit in the center opposite the hapless manager and play our role. Here is how the Agatha situation usually went with a student we'll call Karl:

Agatha: Hi Karl, how's it going? You wanted to see me. What's up?

Karl: Uh, well, yes. Uhhhhh, thank you for coming.

Agatha: I always come when you ask me. What's up?

Karl:	Yes, well, uhhhhh we have a bit of a problem.
Agatha:	Who is *we*?
Karl:	Agatha, I'll get right to the point. I just got a call from a client, one of the managers on the M-2 project at Westco. He uhhh, says there have been some…uhhh… complaints about you and…
Agatha:	Who?! Who called you?!
Karl:	Just a second now. Let me…
Agatha:	What was he complaining about? We're absolutely on track to hit the March code-drop!
Karl:	Well, it isn't the project performance. It's that…well he complained that you don't…he says you have a body odor problem.
Agatha:	(Shrieks) What?! Is he saying I stink?! Is that what he's saying?!
Karl:	He didn't use those words but he did say…
Agatha:	Who was it? I demand to know who it was. I have every right to confront someone who is attacking me and who is trying to destroy my professional image. I'll bet I know who it is. It's Devon, isn't it? He is a weakling and I constantly make him look bad because he comes to meetings so unprepared. It's Devon. I knew he would find a way to get back at me. I'm going to let him know that calling my boss…
Karl:	(*panicky*) Actually, it wasn't just the client. It's not an isolated incident. It has also been brought to my attention by people right here in the office.
Agatha:	Who? No. Don't tell me. Who else could it be but Samantha and Donna? They are quite the team. They have something rotten to say about everyone. I guess

I'll just have to sit my ol' stinky self down next to them and ask them if they want to say something to me directly instead of trashing me to everyone else.

By now it's pretty clear that Karl has lost control of this situation. Usually, I let someone else try but it almost always ends up worse because they toss in some more "relevant" facts and a bit more condescending reasoning. Often they portray an apartheid world of the clean people and the stinky people.

I have actually handled this situation three times in my career. It gets easier each time – at least for me. When someone is accused of being stinky, they *do* feel like it's an apartheid world and they are in a stinky Soweto all by themselves. If you act like you bathe and they don't, it hurts and causes resentment. Everyone bathes. If you become condescending and try to sympathize with their woeful disgrace, they hate you worse.

I saw an episode years ago on Oprah. As the subject of the show, they had a woman who had a body odor problem that she claimed she could not deal with and that she suspected was being used to mask people's real prejudice which was directed against her for being overweight. Even though I was in Seattle and this was a rerun of a show that had been filmed two weeks prior in Chicago, I knew she stunk. When people say you stink, you stink.

They even had an expert from one of the big universities flown in to explain how it is that people who try to deal with their stinkiness sometimes cannot do so. Let me repeat: he was an *expert* on why people might not know they stink. Where do you find *him* in the Yellow Pages? Anyway, his reasoning was that they have a form of anosmia, a condition that occurs when you lose part or all of your sense of smell. According to his theory, when they are in the shower, they don't know when they are odor-free; they just guess and turn off the water. Then they get dressed and go to work where everyone realizes they didn't do a very good job of bathing. I'm paraphrasing here. It took the expert through two commercial breaks to say the same thing. Oprah didn't buy it and she stuffed the guy.

Do you see what I'm doing here? I'm dealing with the wrong issue. If even an *expert* can get stuffed, how are you going to do any better? You shouldn't even try. You're a manager, not some idiot palavering on Oprah. Now let's see how I handle it:

> Agatha: Hi, Charles, how's it going? You wanted to see me. What's up?
>
> Charles: Hi, Agatha. I need to spend some time with you on a bit of a sensitive subject and I want to be very careful not to hurt your feelings. This has nothing to do you're your job performance. I'll get right to the point. You have a body odor problem and you're going to need to address it.
>
> Agatha: (Shrieks) What?! Are you saying I stink?!
>
> Charles: I don't talk to people that way. I didn't ask you in here to insult you; so please don't imply that I am trying to do that. I am saying you have a body odor problem. I don't know why. I don't have any doubt that you are neat, clean and practice great hygiene like any professional. In situations like this I have to think first about the individual – in this case you.
>
> Quite often such issues have a medical basis. Sometimes those medical reasons can be serious such as with interactions between prescription drugs, food allergies, etc. I don't know. I'm not an expert.

	However, it's potentially an indicator of something that might affect your health and, as you might assume, it can affect the comfort of others and I'm sure you don't want that, so…
Agatha:	Have other people complained?
Charles:	The only one even coming close to complaining is me; and I was kind of hoping you would view this as a professional concern and not a complaint. View it as you will, I would like you to consider seeing a doctor and figure out a way to deal with it.
Agatha:	What if the doctor says there's nothing wrong?
Charles:	You still have to deal with it.

Who controlled that conversation? Even when she tried to turn it around in an effort to make me defend myself, I kept control. When she tried to make me defend myself, I put her in the position of accusing me of being insulting and unprofessional.

One of the biggest mistakes the novice manager makes in situations involving a tough issue is to drag the names of other people into the conversation, in order to fortify their position with credible testimony. Never do that. In addition to coming across as weak, you set off a possible chain reaction of personnel situations. It cannot end well. It will certainly end worse than if you just stepped up and said, "Here is the problem, and here's what I want it to look like when you, fix it." This is not a court of law and the employee cannot call witnesses – and neither should you.

The reason I chose the stinky Agatha situation is because it is such a distressing moment socially that you are quickly taken out of your role as a professional. But you can't let this happen. You *are* a professional and you can't opt out briefly when it gets weird or icky.

One last pointer on the Agatha situation. Did you notice that I did not take the monkey onto my back at any point? I didn't even share the monkey. In fact, I didn't even offer the monkey some peanuts. I got it down to a Tarzan level of articulation: "Agatha smell bad. Agatha must smell better."

One more rule for potential monkey-on-the-back types:
If Tarzan can't articulate it, the monkey is heading your way.

If you manage long enough, you will likely run into an Agatha. One that should have been the toughest was the last one I did. I had just been chosen over a woman with far more experience than me for a key management position. They were looking for hard-hitting leadership and she was more of an SOP-type (Standard Operating Procedure). What they needed was some swashbuckling. By the way, more and more of us left-handed, right-brain types were getting into positions of power at that time. Things were tough and the company was looking for some different thinking.

Three months into the job, I was standing next to the woman and my eyes began to water. Then I overheard a couple of people talking about the fact that this woman used excessive perfume. Excessive? I think she was putting it on with a crop duster. On days when the bio-organic layer didn't penetrate all the way to the surface, she smelled like a mixture of baby powder and bug spray.

I laid it out very simply in my summary: "I don't know what's going on but you've got to do something about it." I also let her know that the crop dusting was not working out. That may have been crossing the line but I think I would have died if she had merely tried asking the biplane to make another pass.

Okay, we learned a lot in the Stinky Agatha situation. Let's see how you handle the next one.

EDWARD, THE SEEKER OF JUSTICE.

There are some things that apply across all companies. One of them that is fairly universal is that you cannot use company assets for personal business. You can use the company phone to make phone calls now and then, but technically that's about it.

With that as a background, here's the situation as I put it on the overhead for the students in a middle management class:

Ted is a good manager – one of your best performing managers.

That's why it was a bit unsettling when Edward came to your office with a complaint about Ted.

It happened over the weekend in mid-April. Ted was using the company scanner in Network Operations. He is a CPA and does some tax preparation work on the side. His scanner at home was broken, so he asked one of the Network Technicians if it would be OK to use the company scanner. While he was in there, he also made copies of several large tax returns.

When Edward came into the Net Ops room to get some supplies, he saw Ted at the scanner. Ted looked embarrassed. He quickly gathered all his stuff together and hurried out of the room. Edward came to your office and told you what he had seen. You thanked Edward and said you would look into it.

It's been about two weeks and Edward is here to see you again.

I'll get you started on the conversation and then you try to figure out how to take over. We'll complete the conversation as it usually plays out in my classes. Then, as always, I'll step forward like a hero and have exactly the right answer.

Wilma is the hapless manager I have selected to deal with Edward, who is played by me.

Wilma: Hello, Edward. What brings you by my office today?

Edward: Oh, just a bit of follow-up on the situation with Ted.

Wilma: Is there more information I should be aware of?

Edward: Actually, I was hoping to get some information from you.

Wilma: How so?

Edward: I know that the information I brought to you was disturbing. Using company property for personal business is serious and I know that it can be a firing offense. I know the company doesn't take it lightly. Otherwise, you wouldn't make us sign the company policy book every year. It's serious, isn't it?

Wilma: Yes. We take it seriously.

Edward: Well, Ted acts like nothing happened. I don't get it. Are there only consequences if you're not a manager? I mean, what's this: RHIP – Rank Has Its Privilege? Did he just get off scot-free until next tax season?

[Let's take a break. I never give the student a break but this is a good time to raise a couple of questions. One question is, in general, where do you go at this point? Is using company property a serious violation or not? If using the copier and scanner is just a slap on the wrist, then what are you going to say when people start using the copier for their volunteer groups or bringing in their friends to use the server to play an Internet-based war game with their competitors in Boston?

Is Edward right to suspect that since Ted is a manager, he gets away with misusing company assets?]

Let's resume.

Wilma: All employees are held to the same standard when it comes to using company assets for personal business.

	The fact that Ted or anyone else is a manager or executive does not change the policy.
Edward:	It kind of looks that way, Wilma. It looks that way to me and everyone else.
Wilma:	What do you mean everyone else?
Edward:	Wilma, come on. Everyone knows Ted was caught with his hand in the cookie jar. Let's not play games.
Wilma:	I'm not playing games.
Edward:	Then why is Ted smiling and acting like nothing happened? Is that because nothing happened? If so, when can I schedule the copier and the scanner? My daughter's having a big fundraising thing and I'd sure like to avoid going down to Office Depot to make copies. I mean if Ted got off scot-free, then all bets are off, I suppose. Huh?
Wilma:	Ted did not get off scot-free. No one can go in and use company assets, especially ones that cost real money for usage such as a copier. I dealt with Ted. He paid for the copies and he was told not to do that again.
Edward:	So, every dog gets a free bite. Does that mean, we all get one free pass to do whatever we want and then we just agree never to do it again?

[Pause here. What the heck is Wilma doing? Who's in control here? Where are we headed with all this? But wait – there's more...]

Wilma:	No, that's not what that means.
Edward:	I'm sorry, Wilma. It kinda looks like it does. Look, all I want to know is that the company doesn't make policy and then waive it just because it was breached by a manager. I want to know that I'm working for a company of integrity. I would like to know what

someone should expect if he or she is caught abusing the rule of not using company assets for personal stuff. Personally, I think it ought to go harder for a manager who violates the rules. Did he get anything other than a teeny little warning?

[Wilma now feels as though she needs to show Edward that company policy means something. So how does she do that?]

Wilma: Let's just say, he got more than a slap on the wrist and a warning. We take company policy seriously. Ted understands that much more clearly now. I doubt that he'll be doing that again.

Edward: Or else what?

[At this point, in my role as Edward I get up and leave disgusted. Actually, I didn't have to fake it too much. This had been a dreadful conversation. It was about 90% too long. Let's try it with Charles as the manager.]

Charles: Hello, Edward. What brings you by my office today?

Edward: Oh, just a bit of follow-up on the situation with Ted.

Charles: Is there more information I should be aware of?

Edward: Actually, I was hoping to get some information from you.

Charles: How so?

Edward: I know that the information I brought to you about Ted was disturbing. Using company property for personal business is serious and I know that it can be a firing offense. I know the company doesn't take it lightly. Otherwise, you wouldn't make us sign the company policy book every year. It is serious isn't it?

Charles: You know we take it seriously. What's your point?

Edward: Well, Ted acts like nothing happened. I don't get it. Are there only consequences if you're not a manager? I mean, what's this: RHIP – Rank Has Its Privilege? Did he just get off scot-free until next tax season?

Charles: That's a discussion between Ted and me. It's been handled. Is there something really significant you came to tell me?

Edward: It's just that I was curious what the penalty is for using company assets for personal business.

Charles: We are done with this conversation. And when I say done, I mean this is not a topic of conversation in my office or elsewhere. It has nothing to do with you. One thing I can assure you, Edward, if you ever have a performance issue or find yourself under some type of disciplinary action, I will maintain your dignity with the strictest confidentiality. Are you willing to offer Ted the same degree of professionalism?

The term schadenfreude[5] means: *the enjoyment obtained from the misfortunes of others.* It sounds sick but almost every human indulges in it at one time or another. You can't stop that. But you can chase guys like Edward out of your office. When you take disciplinary action, even in the case where one person has hurt another, the action is strictly between you and the person being disciplined.

You will feel on the spot. You will think that others are wondering if you had the guts to step up to the problem. Too bad. You can't discuss it. You can't even make little remarks like, "Let's just say Ted

---

[5] Pet peeve: Please pronounce the short "e" at the end of schadenfreude. It has four syllables. Philistines and cannibals pronounce it with three syllables.

will think twice before he does *that* again." You can't wink or smile knowingly. Your job is to make sure you have handled it between you and Ted. And then you have to protect Ted's dignity. Why on earth would you want Ted to wander around like a whipped dog?

In some of the role playing, I have had the more creative types say that Ted used three dollars' worth of paper and toner. He has paid that back and agreed never to do it again or he will be fired.

But if you want to know how I would have handled it in real life, my solution probably would have been to say to Ted, "Don't do that anymore."

Lesson learned:

The point of the role play is getting the manager to think like a professional. The manager has to know where to draw the line on subject matter. The manager has to learn to control the conversation and not let it drag on and on. Finally, the manager has to learn not to defend himself or herself. You don't have to pass the employee's test or prove that you have made a wise choice.

It goes back to the concept of WHAT. Remember, the majority of mistakes made by a manager or executive stem from solving the wrong problem. What problem was Wilma trying to solve? – precisely the problem I was unwilling to solve. She was trying to satisfy the employee's curiosity and perhaps assure the employee that she is a good manager.

What Wilma could have done is apply WHAT management concepts to the employee. I've done that often when an employee is bugging me about something that is none of his or her business.

Charles: What problem are you trying to solve here, Edward? Are you trying to make sure I'm doing my job or are you trying to make sure Ted suffers to a degree you think is sufficient?

Things get a little different in the case where one employee or manager has hurt, harassed, or offended another employee or manager. In that case just like the Edward case, the employee will often want to know what happened. They will want to know that their suffering was avenged. If you just brush them off, their next stop might be the attorney's office. On the way there, they will tell everyone what an insensitive jerk you are. What you need to do is show compassion. That's not just our job as managers; that's our job as human beings. You need to know if the hurt person is okay and getting on with things. You ask if there is something that still gives him or her concerns going forward.

If all they want is closure by seeing how the offender was punished, they just need to understand that you don't talk about that. In that case, a quick summary thought is in order: "It has been handled. I'm confident we will all be able to move on."

Now you're ready to work on a tough one. Let's do a compound problem – one that gets more difficult as it goes along. Of course, it can only get more difficult if the manager has an employee who has created a mess *and* the manager is handling it poorly. Since I am playing the problem employee, I will do everything I can to make sure the manager is handling it poorly.

Here's the situation: *Roger works hard throughout the week but due to the fact that he has fairly severe gum and teeth problems, he has to go to the dentist every Thursday around 2 PM.*

The team is right in the middle of a major proposal and they realize that Roger has left with the folder that has all the financial information in it. They come to you and ask if you have a copy. You don't. So you call Roger's home and ask his wife the name of the dentist he goes to every week.

There is a bit of a pause and then she gets you the dentist's phone number. Finally, she asks you if you are really looking for Roger because he hasn't been to the dentist in two years.

Dave is his manager. He asks to see Roger the next day:

Remember, I'm playing Roger. One other note, I'm going to put in a number of pauses to make pointers. If I don't, it will be too long between what happens and what needs to be pointed out.

Roger: Dave, I understand you called my home last night and had a personal conversation with my wife without first informing me.

Dave: Actually, I called because…

Roger: Thanks a whole heckuva lot for making things worse in my marriage. We were just starting to make progress and now she thinks my boss is hunting me down. She thinks you're on my case and she wonders if we're going to be okay financially. Thanks a lot.

Dave: Roger, you know we are right in the middle of a huge proposal. You had information that…

Roger: That couldn't wait until morning? When you call at three in the afternoon, you are essentially two business hours from the next day. What's with the death-march mentality?

Dave: We are all trying to get this proposal out. We felt we needed the information or we wouldn't have called. Now let me ask you a question. You're wife says you haven't been to the dentist in years. Where were you?

Roger: You know I work at least 50 hours a week. I don't understand how taking off one afternoon is now an issue. You never complain when I work late or come in on weekends. I don't get it. Can you show me someone who works more hours than me? Can you show me someone who works harder than me?

[You've gotta admit, I'm terrific at being a pain in the butt.]

Dave: I'm only asking you to tell me the truth. What am I supposed to think when you tell me something and it turns out to be false?

Roger: Are you calling me a liar?

Dave: I'm careful not to call people anything but their name. So where'd you go if you weren't at the dentist?

[Pause: For the sake of sport, I'm momentarily regretting having used this line myself earlier when I was teaching the class about not labeling anyone. I said, "Don't call people good, bad, dumb, smart, lazy, etc. You are to think of them by their first name and refer to them by their first name." Rats.]

Roger: If you must know, I've been having some trouble in my marriage and I...do you really want to hear this?

[Pause: If he hadn't asked Dave the question as to whether he wanted to hear this, Dave could have listened for a while with impunity. However, now that he has started into clearly personal territory that really should have nothing to do with work, Dave must make the decision as to whether he wants Roger's marital problems added to the mix. By the way, employees often go deep into personal problems including addictions, sex relations, etc. Some employees then come back and look for ways to say

you violated a confidence. Regardless of all that, how should Dave answer?]

Dave: I just want to know where you were if you weren't at the dentist.

[Pause: Right answer, more or less. If you don't want to hear about his marital problems, then say you don't. If you leave it open then you might get to play Sigmund Freud later. He should have said sensitively that he didn't want to hear about them.]

Roger: Well, as I say, I've been struggling at home. But I guess that's not important to you. *(Waits for reaction).* So, I've been going to church and...I suppose you don't want to hear about this part, either.

Dave: I guess I just want to know why you said you were going to the dentist when you were really going to church?

   [Pause: If ever there was a time to avoid asking another adult "Why?" it's in a situation like this.]

Roger: Like I said, my marriage has been heading toward the rocks for some time now. *(Starts to sob).* Do you mind if I take a little break and pull myself together?

At this point, I (Roger) get up and leave Dave sitting there. As you might have detected by now, I was going to make this about my marriage, if I possibly could. In a humane company, it is always a safe bet to invoke God, country, or family if you need an excuse. Roger has gotten two out of three into play – mostly because Dave let him.

While Dave is waiting for Roger to come back to the classroom, Clarice, played by my confederate Heidi, comes in to see a somewhat surprised Dave. She reminds Dave of her position on the big project that Dave has been part of.

Clarice: Hi, Dave. I thought I would take a break from the proposal and come talk to you. Do you have a minute? I saw you talking with Roger. I think there is something I should tell you. It's important.

Dave: Okay. But it'll have to be quick.

Clarice: You might not know this but Roger has been having an affair with another member of the project team, Melissa. Every time we all go on a business trip, they always get a room next to each other. When everyone goes out to dinner, they show up for hors d'oeuvres and then one leaves after a couple of minutes and then the other. He has bragged about it to a couple of his buddies. I think that's where he goes on Thursday afternoons. I just thought you should know.

Heidi (Clarice) leaves a completely mystified Dave and I return as Roger. I've been out splashing water on my eyes and rubbing them red to look even more pathetic.

Note that in some companies, Dave might be able to punt this one over to the Human Resources Department. In well run companies, the manager handles all aspects of personnel other than such things as benefits administration and some record keeping. If you are working for a company where HR does the hiring, firing and disciplinary actions, it is probably run by weaker managers and executives than it should be. Of course, those managers and executives would protest such a statement but that's because they have the time to protest, since they aren't really managing.

Roger: Okay. I'm sorry. This has just been a very hard time for me. Anyway, you asked me why I was going to church. Well, it's because I have a bit of a... physical

125

dysfunction and my wife is on prescription drugs to deal with her depression, which I think *I'm* causing.

At this point, I usually turn it over to the rest of the class and I ask if anyone wants to take over for the person who is playing Dave. Occasionally, I get someone who volunteers and then fires Roger on the spot. In reviewing this with other professional managers, they often agree that since Roger lied, he should be fired. Many companies have a zero tolerance policy for lying. Many companies have a policy regarding affairs and trysts but usually it's directed toward affairs and trysts between a manager and a subordinate or non-manager, because of potential lawsuits.

The question is: What should Dave do if he has let the situation get even close to looking like the above? The answer: Suspend the meeting and talk to your manager. If I were Dave's manager, I would not want this goat rodeo to continue for another second. Can anything good happen at this point? You know the answer. We are in pure damage control mode. If you are in a big company like IBM, you and your boss will probably get a high level HR person involved *for advice only* (and a little bit of CYA. They need to be in the boat with you if it looks like it's going to go down). It is still your call – not HR Corporate's call.

Let's redo the call from the beginning and replace Dave with Charles.

But before we do that, let me address the issue of firing. I'll do so in detail in a later section of the book. But let me say here that *firing is a violent act*. It can destroy not only careers but lives, families, college plans, and *marriages*. In the situation above with Roger, you have a wife who is very likely being cheated on; her marriage is very possibly in jeopardy; she is possibly suffering from depression. And now you want to cut off her income!!!???

Some "tough guys" might still say yes, even when I put it like this with all the pain that is taking place. People often like to show how tough they are by demonstrating their ability to endure other people's pain. I respond pretty negatively to such "tough guys." It's visceral.

So send Charles in to play Charles. Roger is now played by one of my other pre-selected confederates who always try to be a more troublesome Roger than I was:

Roger: Dave, I understand you called my home last night and had a personal conversation with my wife without first informing me. Thanks a whole heckuva lot for making things worse in my marriage. We were just starting to make progress and now she thinks my boss is hunting me down. She thinks you're on my case and she wonders if we're going to be okay financially. Thanks a lot.

Charles: Roger, let me make it clear. When it comes to business, I might even call you at your mother's funeral if I think it's urgent enough. Now let me ask you a simple question: You took time off from work to go to the dentist. Did you go to the dentist?

Roger: Charles, I gotta tell ya, I've been having some serious marital issues and…

Charles: I'm sorry to hear that but you didn't answer the[6] question. Did you go to the dentist yesterday afternoon?

---

[6] Notice the expression *the* question, as opposed to *my* question. I am purposely depersonalizing this. If I said *my* question, it could be taken that the reason I am

Roger: No, but…

Charles: How about other times in the last several weeks?

Roger: Well, no. But…

Charles: This is serious. You said you were doing one thing when you were actually doing another thing. You lied to me. You skipped work and you lied to me.

Roger: Charles, you gotta understand. My marriage…

Charles: No. No. I don't gotta understand. If I'm okay with you taking time off to get your teeth fixed, don't you think I would be okay with you taking time off for some other important personal issue?

Roger: It's just that it's kind of embarrassing.

Charles: Please answer the question. Do you believe I would permit you to take time off for a serious issue that you need to deal with, such as a marriage that is in trouble?

Roger: Yes.

Charles: Then tell me how much time you need and we'll figure it out. For now, I would like you to take a week off and work on things on the home front – see a counselor – whatever you feel is right. This is pretty serious stuff you're dealing with. I don't want you to make it worse. Now all that being said, there will be a price to be paid for this. If you were just off playing golf or going to the race track, you might need to look for another job. As it is, you need to take care of the most important relationship in your life.

Roger: But we're right in the middle of a critical proposal!

---

insisting on an answer is because I had a really good question and I wanted an answer to my really good question. It has nothing to do with me. It is the question d'jour. He needs to answer it, regardless of the source.

Charles: Give me the financial information and let's figure out how to hand this off to one of the people on the proposal team and then you go take a week off. If something comes up we can't handle, I'll call you.

Wait a second! The guy lies and he gets a week's vacation?! What is going on?! What about what we learned in the call with Dave, where Clarice came in and explained how Roger was having an affair?

My answer: Do you really consider it a vacation when you get to cool your heels at home for lying? You would have to be one thick-skinned guy to be able to just brush that one off. Imagine how you'll feel the morning you come back to work. This isn't a vacation. But frankly, I don't care if other people see it that way. They have no say. And they are probably really glad they aren't Roger.

As to the new information from Clarice, it's hearsay. But can you ignore it? Not entirely; but you can't act on it directly right now. Just keep your eye on it and deal with Roger. In the future, you will have to address it because you now have information that indicates there is inappropriate behavior. This inappropriate behavior could cause a divorce. You know about it and there will possibly be other trips out of town for the team in the future. When that happens, you will have to sit down with Roger and say, this is what I'm hearing. Do not mention the name of the other party in the alleged affair.

In a way, this goes against the rule of not quoting or referring to the complaints of others when dealing with an employee problem. That rule still exists, if you can possibly adhere to it. However, if you have a problem that is serious and you have no way of getting direct information, then you have to pull the information from others, protect their anonymity and make your pronouncement. When you have the conversation with Roger, you have to admonish him not to go on a witch hunt. Even if you execute perfectly, this is still going to slop and spill all over the place but it will eventually work itself out – or not. You can only do so much.

I'll clean up the ending when the movie of this book comes out. In real life, it ain't gonna happen. You'll be stepping over an odd-colored spot in the hall for a loooonnnnng time.

Chapter Seven
Hiring and Firing
The Responsibility Unique to Humans and Their Shared Humanity

Hiring is a whole long topic and it has a lot of technical twists nowadays. Almost all of these technical twists are either boring or infuriating, so I won't spend a lot of time on them. This could be the subject of an entire book:

But here are just a couple of pointers:

Hiring rule #1:
Only hire "A" players because one "A" player is worth 3 to 5 "B" players and they don't cost 3 to 5 times as much.

Hiring Rule #2:
Never hire anyone without at least one woman interviewing the person.

I learned Rule #2 the hard way. I hired an executive that all of us guys thought was the right person. He was smart, funny, impeccably credentialed and very engaging. About two days after I hired him, Diana, my terrific admin assistant, came in and sat down in the chair opposite my desk. She asked, "So, why did you hire, Kyle?" I explained all of the above in more detail. To this she replied simply, "I don't like him." She then walked out.

This happened a couple more times with a couple other women and I thought that something must have happened and it had started a bit of a ripple effect. Perhaps he had gotten on someone's bad side.

About four months later, I found out something: Kyle was a sneaky and insincere. Women are often better able to spot a jerk.

Even if you don't buy that, there's another, even more important and pragmatic reason to have women interview candidates for key positions, especially those positions that deal with the client. More and more women are moving into decision making roles. In fact, they're already there. If you have a candidate that comes across poorly with women, you have to determine if it's fixable or if it's just not worth the risk.

And if the candidate offends the client, how well is he – or she - going to do internally?

Hiring rule #3:
Make hiring a thoughtful, formal process.

Never be in a hurry to hire. Have at least four people conduct interviews. Make everyone take notes afterwards and put their *unconditional* recommendation in writing; regardless of whether it is for or against the hire. Post-review all hiring decisions at 90 days, six months and a year. Make people *own* their decisions.

Hiring Rule #4:
Don't run for homecoming queen in the interview.

You don't need to prove how wonderfully fun and "with it" you would be as his or her manager.

* * *

The Deserted Island Problem

or

A General Hiring Philosophy to Use the Rest of Your Life

There is an interesting question I ask groups of managers in my classes. Let me set it up. I ask them to take out two pieces of paper, write a fake name on it that they believe is absolutely unique and that hides their identity. I then tell them to be ready to answer two questions which I will ask after painting the situation. Here it is:

You and another person are washed up onto the shore of a large tropical island out in the middle of the Pacific. It was never shown on any of the maps that were on your sailboat before it sank without a trace, many miles away. With your ripped and raggedy clothes as your only possession, the two of you survey the island. It has open fields and in the distance palm trees and other tropical vegetation. There are plants you don't recognize. There is what appears to be a fresh water stream that runs slowly to the sea from somewhere up in the low hills that are in the middle of the island. You have no idea if other people are on the island. Right now, it pretty much looks like you and the other person are the only ones.

Immediately after providing this description, I announce, "You will have 30 seconds to answer the first of these two questions on the first sheet of paper."

Question 1: *What is your objective going to be - not your immediate objectives; but your ultimate objective?*

After the 30 seconds is up, I ask this question, telling them to use the same sheet of paper. They will have 1 minute for this question:

Question 2: *Describe the ideal person to be stuck on that island with you - and please leave out romance or plans for populating the island.*

When I get the papers, the ultimate objectives are almost always the same. The first choice by a long way is to get off the island and back to their homes. The second most popular choice I discount because it's no different than the common objective the rest of us have in the big city and that is to survive. We here on the mainland probably just have an easier job of it.

Some people talk about making a permanent shelter or establishing some type of steady food supply via agriculture, fisheries, etc. But they are usually in the minority and the rest of the class views that as a means to an end and therefore, by definition, not the *ultimate* objective.

After discussing the ultimate objectives, I ignore their descriptions of their island companion. Instead, I ask them to just think about it for five minutes. I ask them to think of their odds of being found right away when there is no trace of their boat and no one even knows this island exists. They are to envision daily life on that island as they work toward their stated ultimate objective.

At the end of the five minutes, I ask them to describe once again, the type of person they want as their companion on that island. Some of the answers change entirely. Most just enhance the first choice they made in the 30 seconds of Round 1.

The simple, short descriptions that I asked for in the first question regarding the kind of companion they would want came down to the following in order of frequency:

- A boat builder (usually about 80%)
- A carpenter (in various morphologies)
- A botanist
- A hunter

There were also the highly clever people who just couldn't resist:

- A servant – and a very meek one at that
- A guy who can make airplanes out of palm trees and albatross feathers
- A guy who can make televisions out of palm trees and albatross feathers
- A fattened cow - preferably a Kobi beef steer

Once we started discussing daily life however, the picture changed entirely. This is someone you have to live with for who–knows-how long. This is someone who will have to hang in there and help solve problems of all kinds. You might have to fight off unfriendly natives or wild animals. Someone has got to get food, determine if it's poisonous, cook it, preserve it, and store it. Does anyone know how to make a fire? Thatch a roof? Make a fish net?

How about a sense of humor? Got any interesting stories? Okay, let's go build a boat. By the way which direction are we facing? Do you know how to navigate with no landmarks? What's that old *European* nautical saying "Red sky at morning, sailors take warning; red sky at night, sailors delight?" That's based on storm directions. Are Atlantic storm directions different than the Pacific?

What if the other guy won't bathe? Will he fly off at the handle when you tell him he needs to?

At IBM, people were often hired under what we called the Best Athlete philosophy. They hired me, a pre-med graduate, over Harvard, Stanford and UW MBA's and PhDs in computer science. Not a lot of use for my organic chemistry and microbiology during my first 17 years at IBM. I saw some of the other guys. They were Brooks Brothers models. I wore one of my father-in-laws old suits to all 7 interviews. We each had great grades. I had a 4 point in my major, some of those guys had 4.0 point overall. Ten of us aced the nasty IBM DPAT test which was later ruled discriminatory and put into desuetude by Corporate Legal and HR. But all of us were in the 95th percentile or above. At that time, they wanted men to have been athletes in one of the major sports. I ran track. None of the guys that interviewed me did. The IBM area manager was on the Princeton hockey team. I got picked for the one opening out of 228 applicants.

So why'd they hire me? I found out later when I was doing the hiring. It comes down to a handful of fundamental characteristics. Sure, everybody has to have good grades and we only accepted applications from a few colleges. There were only 4 in Washington State that qualified. But Stanford and Harvard somehow made the cut in California and Massachusetts.

Beyond that, we looked at the following:

- Communications
- Flexibility
- Adaptability
- Persistence and competitive spirit
- Likability

I have no idea how they determined that but the group of the five top Seattle managers somehow figured it out. I usually need help when hiring because my forte is getting the right people to do the right things but only *after* they've been hired. I can hire former employees and co-workers but I'm a bit below the .500 mark on new hires. (That's a mathematical way of saying I stink at it). It's a great batting average in baseball, not in hiring.

Your job is to ask questions that will help you determine if the person has the 5 traits mentioned above. Numbers 1 and 5 are pretty easy. You need to be creative on the others. Get some life stories. Talk about the hurdles they have had to overcome to get where they were going. Find out what they learned about themselves and if that made them take a new pathway in life. If all the interviewers do that and compare notes, you'll have a good idea regarding fit.

Here's the rule once you've generally qualified the applicant:
Make sure you could see working with the person under every circumstance.

There just might be hurricanes now and then on that island.

You pick the best athlete. The playing field is going to be different at your company than it was where the applicant came from. It is different on a big IBM account than it is in the MBA class at the University. You can't make real life look like your textbook. If you try, you are going to be forever pounding nice round pegs into ugly oval holes.

And you need help when interviewing and hiring. I know I can't do it. I'm too easily fooled.

You see, I have a fundamental problem. I like everybody – at least at first. I have another problem. I think everyone can figure out how to do a job, once they're in it. I think we're all about equally smart. I used to look at my fellow students who couldn't get their calculus homework figured out and I would think they were immorally lazy. How hard can calculus be? Newton already figured it out. We're just regurgitating all of his formulas and they are right there in the book, printed in American English.

It turns out that some people aren't good at calculus. And some people aren't good at what you are interviewing them for. So go back to the rules at the beginning of the chapter. In my case, I would only look at people who had been vetted multiple times. Otherwise, I would hire them all. And later regret it.

FIRING

Firing is worthy of more serious exposition.

Peter Drucker's rule about firing is: Cut it swift and clean.

Peter Drucker was considered to be the world's foremost expert on the subject of management until I wrote this book. But just as Newton had his Einstein, so Peter Drucker has his Charles Herrick.

The truth is, Einstein did not disprove or overturn a single law of Newtonian physics.[7] In fact, Einstein used Newton's three basic laws and never touched a one of them.

When it comes to firing, I would say the same thing as Drucker, with one little twist. Don't fire people, if at all possible. Do a good job of hiring and then work with the people you hire. When you do fire someone, as Drucker said, do it swift and clean.

When you approach the point at which you are going to fire someone, your work to that point should be to show that you did everything reasonable to help the person keep his or her job. Show that he or she clearly did not do what was needed to be done to keep the job, despite lots of notice and offers of assistance.

But like everything else, it's rarely going to be that clean.

The first distinction you must make is whether the person did something that fell short of performance targets or did they break a rule which disqualifies them from continued employment, regardless of performance.

---

[7] Newton never said Force = Mass x Acceleration. He said F = d(mv)/dt. Don't you see? Einstein just refined it with some new stuff on electromagnetic activity. Oh, just shoot me now. I might as well be talking to a wall.

Conditions of Employment vs. Performance Criteria

Conditions of Employment are things such as showing up for work, non-violence, staying sober on the job, telling the truth, etc.

Performance criteria are the things that an employee is asked to accomplish in order to help the company achieve its revenue and operating goals: sell three thousand widgets per month; return all complaint calls within 1 hour; reduce overhead costs by 11 percent.

Conditions of employment are measured by a binary assessment. You are either complying or you are not. Performance criteria can usually be measured across a range. This makes most performance criteria relative and most conditions of employment absolute.

When someone is not meeting their performance criteria, you may put them on an *Improvement Plan* and ask them to build from their current level to an acceptable level. If new orders are at the unacceptably low level of 5 per month instead of 35, you might tell the employee that the number of new orders needs to be 10 for the month of March, 25 by the end of April and 35 by the end of May. This is an improvement plan to get the employee back on track over time. You are looking for *measurably* improved and *sustained* performance.

You would not do such a thing for a condition of employment. If you found out that the CFO had stolen $100,000, you would be unlikely to put him on an Improvement Plan:

"Bill, you stole $100,000 last quarter. Next month, I want your thieving to be down to $30,000 and by the end of May it needs to get back to zero."

If someone crosses the line on tardiness, sexual harassment, selling confidential data to the competition, etc., you act in a binary way. For something like inveterate tardiness, you say no more coming in late.

For selling confidential data, you might alert upper management and then call the police.

Here's the Rule:

> **All companies need to have a written list of *CONDITIONS OF EMPLOYMENT* and an up-to-date *Policy Manual***

And the employee needs to sign them as standalone documents every year.

Policy Question for you:

> **With the proliferation of social networks, networking devices and technology in general, do you have any kind of *written* policy regarding the use thereof, including the Internet**

It's really hard to show consistency in how you discipline or dismiss employees if every manager is making up his or her own rules for what an employee can or cannot do with networking technologies on the job – or anything else, for that matter.

THE APPRAISAL PROCESS

Once a year, most people get their performance review. If it is at all a surprise, the manager did not do his or her job throughout the year. If the lawyers and HR guys had their way, you would do an appraisal every day and the employee would sign off on it in front of a notary or a Federal judge, whichever was more convenient.

IBM used to teach everyone who went to any of its management schools that we were to do quarterly, interim appraisals. I was one of the few people stupid enough to try it. I compounded my stupidity by taking to task the most powerful salesman in the office – almost thirty years my senior. I had felt for some time that he had given up on getting a major client to upgrade their mainframe.

So, I scheduled his interim appraisal and told him the 13 words we were taught to say. "If I were to appraise you today, you would be appraised a __." In our system we had four passing grades and one failing grade:

1 = Far exceeds expectations
2 = Consistently exceeds expectations
3 = Exceeds expectations at times.
4 = Meets requirements
5 = Does not meet requirements

If appraised a 5, you must be put on an Improvement Plan or, on rare occasions, fired outright.

To most employees, only the appraisal ratings of 1 and 2 feel acceptable. It's supposed to be a bell curve but it never is. One of the things the company did to try to make it a bell curve was to confront managers this way: "So, John, all your people are 1s and 2s; yet you aren't achieving your sales targets as a unit. It appears all your people are in the upper percentiles of performance, so *you* must be the problem."

The reason that didn't actually work was because the middle manager who would have given that speech was probably appraising all his subordinate managers as 1s and 2s, just like you were.

Back to my managerial coming-out party.

So, I bring in this imperial individual, who was 6'4" tall and looked like royalty and I give him his interim appraisal. I said, "Edward, if I were to appraise you today, you would be appraised a three."

He stiffened just a bit. He cocked his head and looked at me in an amused way – kind of the way a chicken looks at an ant that's crawling right toward him. He then proceeded to kick my little pink butt all the way up around my ears. I was pinned back in my chair, arms flailing, head turning from side to side, mouth agape. My arms went limp at my sides and there wasn't even a referee to count me out or call a TKO.

I wasn't prepared for what turned out to be a useless bout. If I had a concern about how he was approaching a multi-million dollar upgrade, I sure as heck didn't need to schedule him for a formal meeting to talk about how I was planning to appraise him on everything in his performance plan - three quarters of a year hence! I should have just brought him in and asked the appropriate questions. If I didn't like what I heard, I could make an edict to insist he make a proposal by date X (good luck on that one!) or I could have asked him how he was going to make his numbers if that particular account was not productive.

I finished the next few appointments I had scheduled. I never did another quarterly appraisal and I don't recommend anyone else do one either. Nobody wants an appraisal. Nobody. I was appraised a 1 for the last 9 appraisals of my IBM career and I hated every one of those sessions. They would be scheduled two to three weeks in advance and then you would get to think about how your politics had been with your boss recently. Was he setting you up for a downgrade? Had someone ratted on you lately? About 8 billion petty little thoughts start going through your head.

That should not have been the case. I did not do that to my employees or subordinate managers. I would let them know in the very first conversation where they stood. They would be given an opportunity to push for a higher appraisal by telling them to go back and look at the specific points in their performance plan and supply me with information I needed to be aware of - or that they would like to make sure to emphasize.

142

Here's how I'd do it:

"Fred, let's get together in the next couple of days. I've done the rough workup on your appraisal. You're looking the same as you were ratings-wise last year but there's a lot to talk about. Look over your performance plan and if you have some other stuff you want me to look at more closely, let me know. Otherwise, let's get together and talk over the key points of last year and then we can sketch out something for next year."

What you should do as a manager, is pull your people in every once in a while and talk about where things are. Tell them what looks like it's working. Ask them what the problem is here and there and then give them a mini-assessment on a couple of areas they need to work on. And then say, "Alice, you're doing great." If Alice has an area she needs to fix, tell her that's an area of concern and you'll want to look at it again. Lay out some picture of what you expect it to look like when she's meeting the objectives. Keep it all about performance and results.

And remember, there's a human being on the other end of that conversation. Stony-faced or not, they're having a visceral reaction. Over time, with trust in your judgment and your commitment to fair play, that visceral reaction gets muted somewhat. But it's still there.

One other tidbit: Outside of IBM, I never used ratings numbers again. If it weren't for our legal system, appraisals would be very informal affairs. Your job is to get it as close to that informal approach as possible. You can do this unless you make the amateur error of including discussions relating to pay in your appraisals.

Here's one last appraisal rule:

Never mix appraisals with discussions of salary or bonuses

Everyone knows there's a link. But when you're talking about performance, talk about performance. Remember, you're not managing people, you're managing performance. In fact, it's more like orchestrating performance.

As soon as you mix pay in with the appraisal, that's all they'll be waiting to hear. That's their valuation and evaluation, not some number you assign to their appraisal rating. When you talk about a pay increase (or lack thereof) do it within a couple of months of their appraisal. You can *generally* hit on the subject of performance then, but only at a high level or monothematically.[8]

***

Here's a question as it relates to pay: How closely do you think morale is tied to pay?

You'll find out in Chapter Twelve, at the end of the book.

Side Note on Powder-Puff Appraisals

In the Millennial age, people are starting to give purely happy appraisals, no negatives or disapprobation. It's the self-esteem movement gone corporate. But if you have established a collegial relationship and they know you are trying to help them, then you can talk about anything. Do this. Then conduct real appraisals of performance.

---

[8] I know. I know. This word is only used in music. So when was the last time you listened to a sonata, Mr. I'm-so-offended-I-can't-keep-reading?
Note: The New York Jewish lady who lived across the street from me when I was a kid used to give me hyphenated names like that. One particularly long one was Mr. I'm-too-stupid-to-wear-a-hat-and-put-on-suntan-lotion-when-it's-95-degrees-outside. The names she gave me were usually harsh but often quite informative. Talk about getting an appraisal every day! I don't want to talk about it. It'll make me crazy. Oy. This is like a footnote to a footnote. If Mrs. Schlindwein were here she would call me Mr. I-can't stop-writing-because-I-think-I'm-so-clever-and-there's-so-much-extra-room-on-this-page.

THE IMPROVEMENT PLAN

In the case of failing to meet performance criteria, you would put together an Improvement Plan. This outlines what the employee needs to do in order to move up from his or her performance being rated as unacceptable for continued employment.

An Improvement Plan should always be developed through negotiation to at least some extent. This allows you to learn some of the impediments the employee feels he or she is facing. You might even back off a little. I have.

The other thing that results from this process is that you lower the risk of a lawsuit or at least weaken the case. Some people are going to sue no matter what you do; so you might at least show that you did what you could to prevent the firing.

Before you sit down with the employee, you need to determine in your own mind what the employee could accomplish in the next 30 – 90 days that would fit these criteria:

- It must be measurable
- It must be improved
- It must be sustained

When you think you have it generally figured out, review it with your boss and then the two of you need to decide whether to pull in legal or an HR person. But if you do that. ...

Here's the rule:

Managers make the decisions.

Lawyers and HR people are *advisors*.

Listen carefully to them and then decide. By the way, for the most part, unless I'm given a direct order, bosses are advisors, too. I'm the guy that has to live with any decision I pronounce. Of course you need to be prepared for the consequences when you go against legal, HR and your boss.

I had one particularly dictatorial boss; but like most dictators, he wasn't all that sure of himself. When he would try laying down the law, I would simply say that I saw things otherwise. I would tell him my concerns as to the outcome. I would ask him if he saw that as a possibility as well. I then asked if he was prepared for the results of *his* decision.

His response, and rightfully so, was to tell me I needed to make sure it all turned out right and to make sure bad things *didn't* happen. And then he'd find a way to back off. Had he not backed off, I would have done everything in my powers to make his decision work. That's the system. Anything else is treason in one form or another. But to let a boss push past you and make a bad decision without at least challenging him or her is also a bit disloyal.

Bottom line: Work it out ahead of time with your boss. Personnel problems are not a good time to fight a two-front war.

When you have worked out a set of actions and targets in the Improvement Plan, you must say these words to the employee: "If you do not meet the requirements of this improvement Plan, your employment will be terminated." These words are awful and ponderous but they must be spoken. And they must be written into the plan so that the employee can't claim he or she wasn't warned of the consequences of failure. This is not a drill. This is not a form of punishment. This is business.

Now that you've got everything set up; the employee is on his or her Improvement Plan and you're in regular communication (the timing of which should be outlined in the Plan) what do you do if it is clear the employee is not going to make it, even before the Improvement Plan period is completed? You sit them down, explain it to them and then tell them their employment with the company is over.

146

Prior to this, you will have gotten signoff from all the necessary parties. You will have their severance package ready. You will have all documents ready to sign so the person is not sitting there in your office while you run around doing all the administrative stuff.

They sign. You walk them to the door. You may choose to let them go to their desk but you may want to wait until after hours. You may also want to have security present.

Isn't this gruesome? Doesn't it sound like an execution? What's that person going to say when he gets home to spouse and kids?

So here's *my* rule, as opposed to *the* rule:

Don't fire people.

I have done it enough. Now that I'm older, I look back at almost all of them and I realize I was "justified" from a business standpoint but not as a human being. People who try to separate the two belong someplace where there aren't people. I could have done more. That doesn't mean I should have been a softie and acted like nothing was wrong. In truth, I should have hit harder but kept my gun in the holster. There are so many ways to deal with poor performance besides the death sentence.

I call my philosophy the *Mohammed Ali* approach to personnel management. Those who were around when Mohammed Ali seemed unstoppable, remember the time when he was put in prison for draft evasion during the Viet Nam war. A lot of people didn't understand it at the time but comedian George Carlin said it best about Ali's desire to get back in the ring: "He doesn't want to kill people. He just wants to beat 'em up."

147

I suppose I am now that way about firing people. Most of the time, when someone's done something worth being fired for, you can work 'em over pretty good and put 'em back in the ring. As time went on, I did this more and more and I don't regret it.

Here's a fundamental tenet –an Earthling axiom:

Firing is a violent act.

I believe firing is such a serious and awful thing to do, even when justified, that in a company of less than 1000 people, no one should be fired without the manager responsible reviewing it with the CEO and answering the following questions:

- How is it that we thought he was good enough to hire and now he's not good enough to retain?
- How much advance notice did he get and what was the process you went through to give him a chance to turn around his performance?
- Were there any special circumstances that you should be aware of and that I should be aware of?
- If the person is a minority, female, older, etc. did you recently hire someone to do a similar job and now you're getting rid of the person in a protected class?

When the employee base knows you have this requirement, it adds greatly to their sense of fair play, which translates to their sense of security. Security is the single greatest desire of almost all employees. Make sure you are aware of it and do the things necessary to fortify it.

Firing is painful. People get hurt. Families get destroyed. Marriages fail. College plans die. Childhoods dry up. Do whatever you can to avoid it with someone who really wants to keep his or her job. Dangerous people, cheats and people who just don't care, have fired themselves. Everyone else you work with until they figure out how to get going again – perhaps in a different role, at a different salary, etc.

Tough guys will tell you otherwise. Tough guys can handle other people's pain as though it were a sign of their own manhood. That's not a tough guy. *Real* tough guys do what's right even when they are the ones getting hurt. In the first century AD, tough guys did what they believed and got fed to the lions. The false tough guys tossed the true tough guys into the arena and hurriedly closed the doors before one of the lions glanced their way.

Hire correctly. Train correctly. Put the right people in the right assignments. Address problems early and you won't have to fire anybody.

Exhibit A

On the Subject of Firing

It's worth exploring the anatomy of a firing. It's not like television where people get fired and they walk out to the elevator all pissed off at the jerk that fired them. It's a pretty grim thing. It is always worth asking and re-asking the question: Is this the only way?"

Before we get going with the story, let's look at one final rule on the subject of pushing an employee out of the business:

> Here's the rule:
>
> **If the manager is young or new to management, then you must intensely review the disciplinary process.**

Don't let young managers do it on their own, regardless of what a great learning experience or character builder you think it will be. Make it abundantly clear to the manager that he or she is not even allowed to *start* the push-'em-out process without you there every step of the way.

Here's the story I hope will make it clear as to why.

Mark was in the wrong job. He was a former camp counselor who went to business school and then his dad got him hired by the executive who ran IBM's Salt Lake City office. They were old friends. Salt Lake seems very nepotistic to outsiders but that's the way it often works there. The broader community is tighter knit, if I may be permitted such an oxymoron. Whether I approve or not, it fits in with my tribal-instinct model.

Shortly after coming to Salt Lake, Mark's new manager, Robert, was approached by the person who was then managing Mark. He explained that since Robert was from a more systems-based background, that he really ought to mentor Mark. Besides, Robert and Mark were both in their late 20s and it would be easier to relate. Flattery got him somewhere. Robert, who was new to management, took the bait.

Mark could not sell. He could not draft a proposal. He had no clue as to how to address large business issues with computer applications. He had been protected by his dad's friend the IBM area exec, but now that executive had taken a foreign assignment. Mark's only protector was Robert. Everyone else wanted him gone.

Robert worked hard at it. He stayed late often to help Mark build a proposal or prepare a presentation. He made client calls with Mark that were nothing short of bizarre.

On one call, Robert sat in one of the two chairs opposite the client exec, while Mark went to the far side of the cavernous office and sat with his briefcase on his lap. Both Robert and the exec looked at him with befuddlement but Mark didn't budge. So Robert began the conversation as to why IBM should get the upcoming contract for an automated warehouse. We had pretty much invented them and we certainly had perfected them.

Right in the middle of one exchange between Robert and the exec, Mark spoke up and reminded him that there was some other business we needed to talk about. IBM had a new financial guy in headquarters and he was pushing the field to do a better job on collecting AR. Knowing the subject, Robert held up his hand to halt, letting him know that it wasn't the right time.

A minute later, Mark covered half the distance between where he sat and where the exec and Robert were talking. He placed his opened briefcase *on the floor*, made a few starts at a little speech and then sat down, leaving the briefcase in the middle of the floor.

The exec and Robert looked at each other. They were both dying of curiosity; so they asked Mark to tell them what he wanted. It turned out that the client had bought 2 (as in two) typewriters more than 5 months earlier and had not paid for them. Robert said that was not the subject of the meeting. The new admin manager in Salt Lake was a self-serving tyrant and he had threatened Mark on the subject in order to get rid of two more AR ticky-marks. Mark, always in fear for his job, acceded to his browbeating and was now interrupting a multi-million dollar discussion for the sake of collecting on two typewriters.

Mark never got any better at selling. Finally one day, the executive VP of IBM field operations flew in to let Robert know he was about to be promoted to a position in New York. Robert knew that once he left, the sharks would get Mark. He and Mark had become friends outside of work and often went hiking and cross-country skiing together. He had the conversation he felt he needed to have with Mark.

"Mark, as you know, I came in here with a specific mission and I'm one of the people they are looking at as someone who eventually will run the company. My time is probably short – don't know for sure. How do you think you'll do when I'm gone and you're back working for Glenn or someone being moved up from a staff position in San Francisco?"

"They'll probably fire me right away."

"How sure are you of that? This is very important."

"I think they were getting ready to do it, even before you came to Salt Lake."

"Then if that's what you believe, what do you want to do? Do you want to wait until you're fired to look for another job or do you want to go out there while you can still say you're an IBMer and find a job?"

Mark began to sweat and fidget. Robert tried to calm him down. Mark finally said, in almost a childlike way, "I want to stay here. I like it here."

"Are you capable of surviving?" Robert asked.

"But I like it here."

"Mark, I'll be gone in about 90 days. I'm telling you this as a friend. You have never made your performance objectives. Never. I was overridden regarding your appraisal last year by my boss – your dad's friend. You did not make a single sales objective. But I've got to admit, I did not fight very hard to appraise you a 5. [A 5 = Does Not Meet the Requirements of the job.] And you have actually gotten worse since then. You still haven't sold anything other than that disk drive order I got for you when you were on vacation."

"So what do I do?"

"Once you go on an Improvement Plan, you will have 90 days before either turning things around – which we both know you won't – or you get fired. During those 90 days, you get out there and find a job. Okay?"

"Okay."

"So come in on Monday and we'll set up the Improvement Plan."

That Monday Mark came in and they made a rough draft of an Improvement Plan. Mark agreed that most of it made sense and then he asked if he could take it home to look it over for a while. Mark was absolutely terrified the whole time. Sometimes his mouth was so sticky he had to gulp two or three times to get his tongue free from his soft palate. It was awful.

The next day he didn't show up for work. He didn't come in on Wednesday either. That morning, Robert called and Mark said he was very tired but would be in on Thursday. Thursday morning Robert called again. This time Mark's wife answered and she said Mark couldn't get off the couch. She whispered into the phone. "Robert, what's going on? He won't talk to me about it." She was on the verge of crying. She was a smart, capable woman, a great wife and the mother of a sweet little girl. She just wanted a good family life and now it was coming apart.

The following Tuesday, Robert got a call from Mark's dad. Robert had been over to the family house for dinner on a number of occasions. He had a great relationship with Mark, Sr."

"Robert, can you tell me what's going on?" Salt Lake is a unique environment. Anywhere else it would be considered a violation of privacy and protocol to have this kind of discussion. Robert, though not a Mormon, understood this. In addition to Mark's father's standing as a leading businessman, both Mark's family and his wife's family had the special status of being Pioneer families – descendants of people who came to the Valley with Brigham Young.

Robert said what had needed to be said for the last 3 years. "Mr. Thomas, you know Mark is not right for this job. That should have been apparent in the first year. Now I'm about to leave..." Robert told him the whole story and plan. He then agreed to let Mark stay home for a bit longer.

Mark's father finished with these words, "All I know is that I have a very sick boy."

The following Monday, Robert picked up the phone to hear Mark's father tell him, "Mark committed suicide. My wonderful son is dead." They talked briefly. Mr. Thomas made every effort to let Robert know that he had been doing the right thing and in the right way. He let him know that he had appreciated how Robert had looked after his son so well, so much like a friend as well as a manager. He knew Mark would not have survived this long without Robert acting as his shield.

The weekend prior to that awful phone call, Mark had left before sunup and had gone up into the mountains to stay alone at the family cabin. When it was discovered he was gone, several young men from Mark's church began the hunt. It turned out that Mark had attempted suicide about a year before he came to work at IBM.

Two of the young men pulled into the long driveway along the side of the cabin. Mark raced out the other door and hopped in his car. The two men got back in their car and gave chase.

About a mile from the cabin, Mark's car drifted over into the wide grassy median that separated the two directions of traffic, and coasted to a stop. While driving, Mark had pulled up a rifle, placed it in his mouth and squeezed the trigger.

Robert cried for three days. Frequent visitors came to his office to tell him that it wasn't his fault. Robert had told the branch manager on the Friday before what was going on. Word spread. Robert would listen to each person's explanation as to his lack of culpability. Finally, Robert would just say, "I lost a friend. A wonderful young man died and left behind a wife and child. He was a sweet harmless person and I miss him terribly. I don't feel guilty. I feel sad."

The funeral was huge. Because of the Thomas' Pioneer status, one of the Twelve Apostles of the Mormon Church was scheduled to speak. Speculation roared about town, once that was known. This was a rare thing. Apostles are the next tier below the Presidency – the Prophet. To Mormons, they are capable of saying something that is considered almost scripture. And this Apostle, a friend of the family, was going to have to deal with the issue of suicide, a major sin and one that many knew would prevent someone from reaching Celestial Heaven, the highest level of Heaven in Mormon theology.

The man was a superb orator. He was in his mid-40s, sharp looking and with a commanding presence. Toward the end of his talk, he addressed the issue simply by saying, "I have seen Mark in his new home." He looked about as everyone held their breath. "Mark is going to be all right." A huge sigh went throughout the assembly. Many cried. His mother shook uncontrollably and Mark's father and many terrific brothers huddled about her to comfort her.

Robert got a phone call three days later from Mark's wife. She asked if he would come over and help her with all the paperwork. He spent the next two days sorting through bills, receipts and other documents. In doing so, he came across one interesting piece of paper. It was the information sheet filled out only recently for the new psychiatrist Mark was seeing. Mark had checked off "no" to the many ailments they ask about in your medical history, including the questions, "Have you ever been treated for depression?" and "Have you ever thought of committing suicide?" Mark had been treated many times for depression and he had previously attempted suicide.

***

The story you have just read about Mark is told so that you can see the far end of the spectrum of emotions when someone is fired. Even if Mark hadn't committed suicide, it would have been devastating. Mark was an administrator and should have been given an administrative job. It wouldn't have paid as well but he would have been much happier.

Instead, Robert moved on him to force him to go to another company. To do what? Was there no fit for him at IBM in Salt Lake? There certainly might have been. Robert would have had to fight a lot of people to make that happen and he might have lost but that's what should have happened. Mark had even hinted at it and Robert, focused on the task at hand, went for the move with the greater degree of difficulty. He wanted to go through the appropriate Improvement Plan and then cut it swift and clean.

There are still those who see Mark as a sad case but then they say, "That's business." They would do it that way again and they really don't mind firing people. In fact, the story of Mark would be a good one to tell the other tough guys over a Scotch.

But if they said it so cavalierly to me, they might not fare so well. My full name is *Robert* Charles Herrick. I pushed Mark to leave the company. He killed himself. He will not see his daughter graduate from high school. He will not see her get married. He will never again see a sunrise nor his sweet wife. I had a hand in that.

Do whatever you can to avoid firing people.

Summary Statement on Firing
Why This Book is Different from Other Management Books

In reading the pre-release of this book and this section on Mark Thomas in particular, a number of people have come back to me and said they now understand why I am so much against firing. Below is my response to that, which not only incorporates the subject of firing but which reveals the germinative principle behind much of what I advocate for the treatment of our fellow Earthlings:

Here is the actual wording from a reply I sent to a friend and colleague who had emailed me after reading about Mark:

Mark is one of the reasons I don't believe in firing people but not the main reason. I think companies should be structured and cultured in such a way that they are built more thoughtfully and carefully and then kept together in a familial – or at least tribal fashion. It feels way more normal to the human spirit.

What we have now is artificial and designed for war which we can handle for a brief period of time only. It is very hard on humans.

People desire innately the benefits of family and tribe. They want the traditions, culture, and meaningful roles. They want to be part of a community purpose, which they know will change from "season to season." But most of all they want the security that comes from permanently belonging and the comforting awareness that they are being led by people who are both competent and noble.

This is the point to which we Earthlings must return.

Section 3

Operational Management

(Focusing on the business ... now that you're not such a beast)

Chapter Eight
Hierarchical Management
And how we got here

So who came up with this idea that there's a CEO, a bunch of VPs, then a bunch of directors, middle managers, first line managers, etc.? At the "bottom" of the hierarchical pyramid are the employees. These are affectionately thought of and often referred to as: grunts, headcount, FTEs (Full-Time Equivalents), etc. In fact, they are often thought of as "et ceteras."

When the concept of the corporation was advancing rapidly in the 1800s, it was clear that the old proprietor-style of governance was not going to work. Even a large factory in the dawn of the industrial era was run by the owner and everyone reported to him. His go-between managers were more like henchmen, reminiscent of the Sherriff of Nottingham's lackeys. Of course, the factory owner's son trumped all unless someone found a way to push him into fast moving machinery, thereby eliminating that layer in the protocol.

The question our 19th century forebears had to answer was: How should a large company manage to communicate its directives organizationally? Were there any models in existence at that time that a large corporation could pattern itself after? There were two: The Catholic Church and the US Army. Both were hierarchical. But the tighter, more familiar formation of the army model won out. Many of the corporate ilk had served in the military so it made imminently good sense to them. The Commanding General lays out the campaign strategy and picks the site for the battles and the subordinate generals line up the battle plan with his approval. The colonels take their regiments and coordinate between the other regiments and then organize via their captains who move their lieutenants into place. The lieutenants then line up all their grunts, headcounts, and FTEs to shoot and stab the opposing grunts, headcount and FTEs. Nothing's really changed in a hundred fifty years.

Somewhere in there are majors and corporals and sergeants. I should know but by the time I was fit and ready to join the Army, we had temporarily run out of wars, so I don't fully understand the structure. It just seems to work.

Actually, one thing that has changed slowly but significantly over the last century and a half is the basis on which power is exercised. In the army, you did what you were told in a battle or you got shot. You couldn't even quit. About halfway through your take-this-job-and-shove-it speech, you would be loudly interrupted. In 19th century corporate America, we moved from the evil industrialist proprietor and his meddling son to militaristic corporate managers who had the power of financial ruin over the workers below them. Reaching past a manager to get at the people below him was (and is) not uncommon, in fact it was a daily practice. The military was not only better organized, they were (and still are) more professional.

Now, jobs are relatively more abundant and employees no longer have to choose between growing rutabagas on a hardscrabble plot of land or standing on an assembly line. During non-recessionary periods, employers have to compete for good employees. They can't threaten to kill them or throw their families out on the street.

So what is the basis for command if you can't cause massive fear each time you walk by? The answer is: Who knows? Mostly we are now just creatures of cultural heredity. *We* do as *they* did, with a couple of modifications each half-generation or so.

When I was growing up, old-timers used to remind me, "When the boss says jump, you ask, 'How high?'" By the time we Baby Boomers had passed it off to Generation X, the response was greatly attenuated.

Today, Gen-Xers build the boss an avatar: "Here you go, boss. Now when you want someone to jump, just hit *run//C*: and click on *this* guy. He'll jump and do all kinds of crap. You'll feel better and you won't have to bug me when I'm working."

I suppose it depends not only on the company but also on the individual managers. Since most managers don't have management training before they become managers or while they are managers, they treat their employees the way they got treated by their bosses or they act like a boss they saw on TV.

At a relatively young age, I was 'discovered' when I was back at IBM headquarters. This was just before the beginning of the company's long slide downward prior to being rescued (*financially*) by Lou Gerstner. What was discovered about me was that I had the ability to articulate a left-handed solution when others were just stepping on the gas pedal harder and getting nowhere. I could also write speeches and glorious executive letters. On numerous occasions I was asked to drive from my office in midtown Manhattan to White Plains just to write a letter. I was handy to have around and often sat in meetings where I was several levels below everyone else in the room. And people actually wanted to know what I thought. I didn't even shave every day. Seriously.

One of the most important beliefs of IBM's founder Thomas Watson was Respect for the Individual (RFI). This tenet along with superb customer service and taking care of the shareholders were known as the Three Basic Beliefs. They're good ones and actually *can* be universally applied to all companies including Exxon, the ice cream parlor and the gambling casino.

I saw a change in RFI at IBM starting in the early 80's. In a company that was blowing away the competition and surpassing its goals, out of sheer momentum it seemed, a discovery was made. You didn't have to lead effectively as a manager (one of the 7 fundamental beliefs of IBM); you merely had to *look* like you were leading effectively. If you happened to be in one of the places where business just wasn't happening, such as oil-depressed Houston in 1983, you were likely not going to pull this *look* off so easily unless you were heavily sponsored by a high level executive before you got there. But increasingly for the rest, what you needed to do in order to get ahead was:

- Have "the look"
- Say the right thing
- Make a presentation to the right people
- Have a sponsor
- Do something for your boss so that he too would be able to take credit

This sounds like a cynical oversimplification – and it is. Most of IBM ran on traditional merit-power, especially outside of the marketing divisions. However, all you need is for enough of the *looks-good* types to crowd out some of the *does-good* types and the ship begins to list.

In the treatment of people, IBM was becoming just a bit like other companies and the RFI belief was starting to be a burden. It eventually was too late to save the company "spiritually" and all that could be done was save it financially. Enter Lou Gerstner.

I was given the honor as a young staffer to make a presentation to a crowded room of people consisting of *every* manager and executive in headquarters. The presentation was called the "Back to the Field" program. The presentation came off great. But I was sick to my stomach when I realized what was really happening. We were going down. The Third World potentates would thrive because, remember, it is better to rule in hell than to serve in heaven.

Relatively speaking, and that is mostly how power is measured, they would be just as powerful and just as well paid regardless of the health of the company.

To me, the signal that something was wrong occurred a few weeks before the presentation. Back-to-the-Field meant they were going to pay all the expenses for anyone in headquarters to go to a field office and be a salesman, engineer or administrator in an employee, managerial or executive capacity. Everyone was eligible and no manager could claim his or her employee was irreplaceable or in any way prevent the employee from going back to the field. How could we justify such a move, financially or from an image standpoint? IBM had never laid anyone off except for 9 people who were accidentally laid off by a manager in the 1930s who didn't know there was a full-employment practice at IBM.

We had to preserve the full-employment practice, we thought; but how do you explain cleaning out headquarters and loading up the field offices? This is where I began to suspect something was wrong. I sat in a meeting that included the new president. He talked about the need to provide superb coverage to the customer. Good so far. And the way we were going to do that was by getting more "arms and legs" out into the customer accounts.

Arms and legs? What about minds and hearts? Soon everyone was talking about arms and legs.

I have to be careful here not to sound too politically correct. I believe political correctness and the scrutinizing of every word to see if it might be offensive is killing this country and giving power to critics, pundits, and lawyers instead of real leaders. So I don't want to leap at the chance to be offended. But it bugged me.

I also have to be careful not to overstate my position in IBM. I was involved in many such meetings but I was not a big player. I eventually took the Back-to-the-Field movement myself, turning down an unheard of 3-level promotion in Howard Greenwald's prestigious directorate. My wife was showing signs of the disease that killed her mother, grandmother, aunts, etc. It was a particularly pernicious variant of polycystic kidneys that killed a person with an aneurism long before she realized she even had the cysts.

We returned to Seattle and I called Dr. Belding Scribner, Professor Emeritus and one of the inventors of hemodialysis. I had worked in his area at the UW Hospital when I was a pre-med student. He agreed to take on one more case and my wife went through various studies. It turned out she did not have the disease, thank God.

I was now free to resume my career but I didn't feel like moving. I stayed in Seattle where I rose to be the head of the consulting group. It was a great position and it later allowed me to move on to be the CEO of a company with thousands of employees and contractors.

But I was mostly an observer in the last days of IBM, including our first official layoff. I laid off my assigned 35 people, helped find a bunch of them jobs elsewhere in the company and then I quit. IBM wooed me back with a number of promises. The person who made those promises later quit on the last day of the program during which you could take the benefit package. I returned from a trip to Denmark where I was working through a problem with a subcontractor for a huge project we were running at Boeing. I arrived home three days after the program expired. I called the exec who had made me the promises, told him what I thought of him and quit again. I then ran a coffee company for three years. Bliss.

I was mostly an observer when it came to the upper echelons at IBM. But I am a really good observer.

However, to observe productively, you need to have a model by which you can make sense of the things you observe.

It was during this time that I developed the what-vs.-how rule. It complemented IBM's solid management practice of focusing on performance results and not on management of the person when you are managing and appraising. But it goes beyond that. Performance-vs.-person is just a corollary of the what-vs.-how philosophy. Both say you need to focus on the issues and not on the personalities. But the what-vs.-how philosophy goes far beyond people management. It encompasses the way decisions are made and communicated. Even more important, it forces the CEO to figure out what business the company is really in and what it needs to do to stay healthy and make progress.

Theory:

If the CEO knows what to do, then his execs can know what to do and so forth throughout the organization

The question then becomes: what kind of management process must be put in place to ensure that each level of management is focused on what must be achieved to meet the objectives of the next level up and ultimately the company?

Of course, what you hope to avoid is the common phenomenon of one level of management aiming for a set of objectives, which when achieved, don't effectively further the goals of the next tiers of management up the hierarchy. Toward the end of the great slide at IBM, one year the field far surpassed their targets but headquarters was in the hole a couple billion. Oops.

The execs who had managed their careers better than they managed the business had lost the spiritual battle. They couldn't urge their grunts, FTEs and armzandlegs to do one for the Gipper. They had to bribe the field.

Here's the rule:

When you lose your people's hearts, all you have left is the cash nexus

Lou Gerstner was brought in from the outside – Amex, a financial company. He felt that he had inherited a faltering entity with little life in it, so he managed mostly the cash nexus. He did great. IBM spun around and was still going strong later under a lifelong IBMer, Sam Palmisano. I met Sam a couple of times at Division HQ. He was one sharp guy. If he had inherited a company with its spirit intact, it would still have its spirit intact. But the body was blue when he got it from Gerstner. Lou had hooked up the lightning rod to the electrodes on its neck and the company climbed off the operating table, big and powerful. But it will never again have a soul.

* * *

Can we pick a date of death for the real IBM? Yes – at least we can get pretty close. A friend of mine who was still at IBM at the time told me about it. It was 1999 when Lou instituted the new order. Managers showed up at various meetings, usually at or near IBM headquarters, where they were introduced to the new hierarchy of Earthlings and their relative importance to the company. (Shades of the movie *Office Space*).

The person running the class put up on the screen, three groups of people in the following arrangement:

Employees
Customers
Managers

He explained that this had been IBM's hierarchy in the past with the employee being the most important to the company. This was wrongheaded in Lou's opinion. The way it should be is:

Customers
Managers
Employees

This looks kinda Third World to me.

This is not only ill-advised to say out loud, it's unnecessary. And it's wrong. Speaking as a right-brained, left-hander, I can tell you this is the kind of linear, two-dimensional stuff we really hate. It's not a straight line and since there are Earthlings involved who have emotions and certain fragile sensibilities, it is not two-dimensional. There's a Z-axis. Don't they see it? Don't they at least sense it?

I'll wipe the foam off the corners of my mouth and work my way back to the point. So, if it's not a straight representation, what figure am I thinking of for relating the three groups of people? A bowtie. On one side are the customers. On the other side (lest the bowtie look like the flag on your mailbox) are the employees. The little knot in the middle keeping it all straight consists of the group known as managers. When you have finished your knot, look in the mirror. You want to make sure one side isn't bigger than the other.

To *ever* tell your employees they are less than Number One – let alone tell them they are number three (note: in a column of three that's the bottom) is pointless and wrong. Your job as CEO and managers is to take care of the company – the tribe. Your company consists *only* of your employees and their families. The best way to do that is to keep the company vibrant and growing. The best way to do that is keep the customer happy. But it's not either/or. And it's not black and white. I have demoted employees for failing to take care of the client and I have fired clients for mistreating my employees. I have also taken managers out of management for pounding on employees. Rock, paper, scissors – not employee apartheid.

Was Lou's hierarchy so constructed because the customer writes you checks and you are burdened every two weeks writing checks to the employees? Yes, armzandlegs are expensive. Most valuable things are. But they need to feel valuable; so don't say demeaning things. If the direction that checks flow is the determinant, my boss is more important than my kids. And, for a moment, so is the guy who bought my used lawn mower.

This is all just my opinion but I watched a small *family* of 400,000 people turn into a great big *company* of 250,000. Virtual offices full of virtual officemates with docking stations are lifeless. You may think you're saving money with shared desks and laptop docking stations but the real top line…

*

Now that you have your organization established with multiple tiers, how do you keep everyone lined up from tier to tier, from the CEO to the men and women on the front lines? How do you avoid misalignment? How can you push an initiative through the ranks – quickly if the company still has a soul, but effectively even if it doesn't?

What is parallax and how do you avoid it?

172

We'll discuss what I call organizational parallax or misalignment of mission and focus. However, what you have to know first is the biggest WHAT or you will either be hopelessly misaligned or aligned on entirely the wrong things.

The first big WHAT I always ask a CEO and his executive team is the following:

WHAT business are you in?

Here's a hint: It's almost *never* what you think it is or what you have already named the company.

Chapter Nine

What Business Are You *Really* In?

Here's an easy game, which you might have played before. Just match the company name on the left with the business that describes it on the right:

1. Harley Davidson		a. The copier business
2. Xerox		b. The housing business
3. Homebuilders		c. The coffee business
4. Starbucks		d. The motorcycle business

Do you sense a trick question – one with four parts, to be exact?

If you matched any of the companies on the left with *any* of the business descriptions on the right, you flunked and joined the group that makes up about 90% of today's executives.

Is the exercise of matching a company with a business description important? It is deadly important and most often not discovered until your competition has rolled past your perceived unassailable Maginot Line and is eating your lunch on the Champs-Elysées.

I'll give you the answers to the four companies' business descriptions in a minute but let me work through an example first from a real live company.

Back in the 70s there were non-profit companies that sold Health Insurance, primarily Blue Cross and Blue Shield. In some states they had merged Blue Cross/Blue Shield companies but in other states like Washington, they not only had not merged, there was a Blue Shield for just about every county.

These companies were run by people who actually *liked* working for a non-profit. Since they weren't in the business to make money, then what they were really there to do was to have a job. This was fine at all levels until people like the *for-profit* insurance companies showed up and started taking market share.

This sent the executives of many of the Blues into a panic. It was okay to be unprofitable but it was *not* okay to go out of existence because it was likely they would lose their jobs.

The CEO of one of the larger of these organizations brought in IBM to do one of our standard executive planning sessions. We did these free of charge, hoping the client would continue to buy our computers at $5 million per copy. Toward the end of a product cycle, big IBM mainframes were highly profitable, which more than covered a one-day planning session, *plus* sandwiches.

Ray Hitchcock was the highest ranking Consulting Systems Engineer in the Northwest at the time. He was one of these people that had an aura of genius, mostly because he was a genius but also because he wore great big eyeglasses that looked like he was gathering data from all over the universe. He also had a cool voice that sounded analytical, even when he was just ordering french fries.

I was barely out of college but I was already showing promise and Ray took notice of me. I had recently been asked to assist in the financial justification of our giant laser printers – the ones where you inserted a tree at one end and paper was spat out the other end at 20,000 lines per minute (seriously). It was an amazing device, but in the days of impact printing, carbon copies, and colored forms, a single copy, black-and-white laser image was being questioned. It sometimes took up to six months of forms analysis to justify one of these. I was still a trainee whose time was less valuable, so I was asked to help out in one of the justification efforts.

This looked really boring. So I did what I always do when a right-handed person tells me how to do something. I sat down with the project lead and asked, "*What* are you trying to do?" She pulled out four giant notebooks with forms in them and explained how they were going to compare the cost of producing each print run on a laser printer against the old impact printers which could still pound on forms hard enough to produce five copies.

I sat alone for an hour with the books, found the biggest print jobs and justified putting in two printers on these jobs alone. Within a year, they had several of these behemoths at Pacific NW Bell and I was a hero. I got a thousand dollars. The *real* people who had watched me justify the printers got to go to Florida. I was pissed. But since I was planning to quit and go to medical school anyway, I smoldered quietly. Business is icky.

Ray Hitchcock knew what had happened and started sponsoring me. He came to me with an offer to participate in the strategic planning process for one of the healthcare companies. I accepted.

We walked into the room with the CEO and his six executive VPs. After going through the agenda for how we would determine vision, mission, etc., etc., he asked everyone to do a little task. Handing out yellow pads and #2 pencils to all seven executives, he asked them to write down in a couple of sentences what business they were in.

As you might have guessed, we got seven different answers. These people at the top of the company were running seven different businesses, yet they ate in the same lunchroom like they were friends and co-workers.

The descriptions ranged from terse: "We are in the business of providing insurance coverage for people's medical needs" to floral: "We are in the business of ensuring that those in need of healthcare will always have access to the quality of care they need and deserve in a fast-moving world where technology is rapidly being brought to bear on problems that have plagued mankind for millennia."

Ray read them all aloud. Surprisingly, they all felt that the seven answers were just fine.

Ray said that he didn't agree with any of them. Lips curled. Words got less and less tactful. I had seen the lunch menu and I began to be concerned that I wasn't going to get the seven-course spread that had been ordered up. These were the kinds of lunches that helped keep the company classified as a non-profit.

Ray was not concerned. He was right and they were wrong.

Determining what business you are in comes about via a branch of consulting called "Functional Consulting." Now that I look back, it was essentially an analysis of WHAT. What business are you in? What do you need to do to be successful in that business? What functions need to be in place to allow you to achieve your mission? And so forth.

We spent a half a day arguing over what business they were in. It reached a paroxysm when Ray asked the executive who had written the floral description to read it aloud again. When he finished, Ray asked him what the difference was between their company and the Mayo Clinic. To each thing the exec said, Ray answered, "The Mayo Clinic does that" or the one that really made them mad, "My wife does that when one of my kids falls down and skins his knee. Are you competing with my wife?"

Mercifully, by lunch, Ray had convinced them that they had to look at the business from the standpoint of a customer, an employee, and a competitor. And, whereas it was nice to tell people at a cocktail party that you were in the business of insuring people's health, the truth of the matter is that you are in............the claims processing business. None of those guys wanted to go home and tell their wives that they were in the claims processing business.

However, Ray convinced them that if they got their 90-day backlog down to 30 days and if they handled all claims thoroughly and correctly on the first pass, Metropolitan Life and the others would find it much harder to compete with them. If they designed their strategy, from marketing to adjudication, around the high-speed processing of claims, their customers would be ecstatic, their employees would know what the priorities were and they would beat the competition – especially the ones who thought their job was to "assure those in need of health yadda, yadda, yadda…"

We spent the rest of the day laying out a fairly simple, high-level strategy for the claims processing business. That company emerged as a premier health insurance company in the Northwest for decades.

By the way, it takes several big computers and peripherals to get your claims down from a 90-day backlog to a 30-day backlog.

And lunch was superb.

So, what businesses are the aforementioned four companies in? And does it really matter as much as it did for the health insurance company I just described?

In the 70s, Honda, Kawasaki, Suzuki and Yamaha were producing great motorcycles and Harley was down to about 23% market share in the big bike arena. Harley Hogs were giving way to four-cylinder Honda 750s, which were faster, smoother, less expensive and more reliable.

But there was one thing Hondas were not. They weren't Harleys.

Harley Davidson made the mistake of thinking they were in the motorcycle business when they were really in the nostalgia-on-two-wheels business. When they figured that out, they changed how they sold the bike. Soon, Harley went from 23% market share to where over 50% of the heavyweight bikes that were sold were Harleys. In fact, to make sure that no one could be like a Harley, in 1994 they even patented the exhaust sound of a Harley. Hogs ruled.

What about Xerox? They thought they were in the copier business. As a result, they were racing with the Japanese firms to produce the fastest, cheapest, most reliable copiers and they were getting their brains beat out. So what went wrong and then what went right?

What went wrong was the idea of competing with the nation which has the world's greatest manufacturers to see if you could out-manufacture them. The Japanese government actually *wants* their businesses to succeed. Our government, led by Jimmy Carter, wanted to split the goose open and get the golden tax eggs. So who do you think was winning: the Japanese Keiretsu or the American company trying to convince the IRS that business lunches should be tax-deductible?

What went right was another functional planning session which said that Xerox was not in the copier business. Customers wanted more. Yankee ingenuity could give them more. The Japanese may be great manufacturers but in the 70s and 80s they were not the inventors. Americans were.

So what was their business? Xerox was in the document management business – and they are still in the document management business. There is a lot more to managing documents than spitting out copies. When they figured it out, they re-emerged with vim, vigor and thew[9] – not to mention massive market share. They even invented a way of looking at multiple documents at once, working back and forth on a computer screen. It was called windowing. They knew how to manage documents; they just weren't

---

[9] Look it up. I tossed this in for the professors and academics because I've been pounding on them so much. They don't know what the word means either but they'll start using it pretty soon.

very good at capitalizing on their patents. Enter other large software firms for soup d'Xerox at the Champs-Elysées.

How about an easy one? What business are companies in that build houses? Give up? If you think it's just house building, think again. Most of the companies that build moderately priced homes for middle class home buyers are in the business of dealing with government regulations. Everything they do is based on financing; financing is based on timing and timing is based on how quickly they do all the studies for wetland, soil, arbor, wildlife, storm water, etc.., etc., to get the plat approval, provided there are not too many neighborhood or community appeals. When an Environmental Impact Statement is required, they often must count the number of frogs and toads. I'm not kidding. Toad-counting is expensive and hard. Actual construction is easy. Coaxing an activist bureaucrat is maddening.

In San Juan County, where I am planning to build a home, it takes a few months to get a building permit. This is very fast compared to other regions in the Northwest - the Seattle area, for example. However, thirty years ago, you applied for a permit in the morning and picked it up in the afternoon. And somehow those homes are still standing, despite the short permitting period.

How many small, independent home builders do you think can survive thousands of dollars of studies, legal actions and delays? The business has changed. Pounding nails is the last thing you think about.

Higher-end home builders are in the habitat business these days. They must create a self-contained, energy efficient, eco-groovy abode or they risk cutting out a considerable portion of the market. Buyers in this range want to walk in the front door and only have to hop in their Prius to leave every once in a while. They want to watch movies in their own movie theater. They want hallways that are 52" wide and ceilings that are 10' high. I went on a Street of Dreams open house tour a couple of years ago and I was shocked at how big even the laundry rooms were. To justify these palaces, builders have to give the owners a face-saving out: energy efficiency to reduce their carbon footprint. (Will we still say *that* ten years from now? I feel like I'm using disco-speak already). So when someone looks at their foot, which is the size of Shaquille O'Neil's, they can say, "Yes, it's a size 23 – but it's a 23 *narrow.*"

How about Starbucks?

After I left IBM, the guy who used to be IBM's head honcho for the Northwest asked me to consider joining his son's coffee company as a one-third partner. The company was losing lots of money. Their flagship store, with cherry wood and brass interior was in Gig Harbor, Washington. It was called Austin Chase Coffee.

It was easy to turn around. The two partners simply were not managers. We fixed a few cost items (e.g., three baristas in the dead afternoon shift became one barista) and all of a sudden we were gushing money. Just about the time we were running out of pockets to stick our cash into, the store burned to the ground and wiped out seven other businesses in the mall. I then got to meet the first wave of emergency lawyers to descend on Gig Harbor. I finally found those new pockets to stuff all that cash into. To our great relief, the Hartford Insurance Group and claims adjustor John Dill came through. We survived and expanded tenfold in less than two years before selling to Caffe Appassionato (like Beethoven's Appassionata Sonata, only it's spelled different – must be a coffee thing).

Austin Chase was started about 5 years prior to me joining the company. About three years before I showed up, Starbucks opened a Gig Harbor store in a new mall that was in a slightly better location. Forget coffee; location is everything. We had cherry wood and brass, curved oak ceilings, and pine floors, whereas they had a somewhat better commute position. But not *that* much better.

When I first got to Austin Chase, I asked the founder what business we were in. He said, "The coffee business." It took all day, but I showed him we were in the morning treat business. When someone came in for a cup of coffee or a latte, they were giving themselves a little treat, a break from another harried day. How were we enhancing that?

Here's how: Good location; great coffee, fast moving lines, gorgeous gals (no ugly old guys with earrings – sue me!) prices rounded off to the nearest quarter with tax; little punch cards that tossed in a free muffin now and then, an honor system for drip coffee where you just put your dollar in a big jar on the counter, poured yourself a cup of coffee and started drinking – no lines.

At any given time in the morning, the place was packed. Because we knew what business we were in and we acted accordingly. Going to Austin Chase was a treat. We were winning.

But soon things changed for everyone.

The thing that made it all change in the coffee world was the fact that Starbucks had figured out what business they were in and then they had raised the capital to take advantage of a great strategy. Many of us who were on the wholesale side selling roasted beans to other coffee shop owners had discovered what Starbucks had known for some time. We had seen which shops were doing well and which were floundering. But with capital and excellent execution, Starbucks had already made their move and had taken off like a rocket, leaving everyone else in the dust. I had moved back to hi-tech by that time but it was fun to watch - and so was their stock. Howard Schultz was a superb executive.

What was the business? It was the best-coffee shop-*location*-in-the-local-area business. In keeping with the theme of a morning treat, Starbucks located their shops in such places where it was easy to get to because - and this is important - you were already going there or at least going *by* there. If instead, you picked a spot that was a *destination* location, you were in trouble. If someone had to hop in their car and drive to your shop, park, get out for the sole purpose of buying a cup of coffee, then you were making it a very expensive latte. When Starbucks, on the other hand, put their shops next to Safeways or other grocery stores or actually *inside* of a grocery store, you were already there; so just go grab a cup of coffee and go shopping. The same strategy worked in metropolitan areas. Locate next to several buildings with thousands of people working in them. Talk about people needing a treat!

In some places, there were two or more Starbucks within a hundred yards of each other – sometimes opposite corners of the same street intersection.

They had a good strategy, lots of capital, and the best real estate teams in the business for finding the right locations. They knew WHAT they had to do and put all their fire power behind it. They knew their Normandy coast. And just like Ike, they didn't send two frigates and a garbage scow to go check it out and see if the Germans had it in 'em to hold the beaches.

So now, fifteen years later, what business is Starbucks in? They are actually getting rid of shops. They're hanging on to the ones in great locations (as defined by in-store sales) and they are still adding shops around the world, but what are they going to do next?

You see, companies don't grow in an upward ramp with little jiggly saw tooth marks adding texture to an otherwise straight line. They grow in discrete stair steps. They go along just fine for a while and then they hit a wall. They have a problem they have to solve to get to the next plateau. If they don't solve it, they stagnate. Sometimes, especially in startups that are growing fast, they have to change out the management team because the executives were okay with 50 employees and one office but at 250 employees they were struggling and at 500 or 1000 they would likely fail. If a CEO like Bill Gates has the capital to surround himself with a good team and if the product is very strong, the top folks can hang in there, but typically other managers in the upper ranks need to be turned over.

Other walls that are hit occur when opening remote branches, expanding the product line from being a one-trick pony to a new product possibly needing capital for R&D. They may need to add a completely new line of business such as professional services. Their warranty and repair infrastructure may need a massive overhaul. There are lots of walls out there.

I took over at STAR Consulting when the management simply could not handle organic growth and the prospective buyer knew it. They wanted someone who could manage potentially thousands of employees and more locations. And there I was with a big sappy smile on my face not even asking for stock options, growing a 700 person company at 74% in the first year.

Let's go back to Starbucks. Maybe they think they are in the coffee ambience business. They also emphasize a lot of humanitarian things. Starbucks is using their ubiquitous chain of stores as a place to tap people on the shoulder for a lot of worthy causes. They use fair trade coffee which actually makes a difference in the lives of coffee farmworkers. But unfortunately that doesn't mean much to a lot of people buying lattes.

They play jazz music[10] and I suppose I should act like I'm cool and into it but I'm not. To me jazz music sucks. And I know a lot of other people who don't like it. So now there are a number of us closer to tolerating our visit to Starbucks than we are to enjoying it.

Don't they realize what has happened? As with all retailers, their ambience periodically needs a new look and I'm sure they have teams working on that, as they should. But don't they first need to figure out *why* people are coming to their coffee shops before they figure out *what* it should look like when they sit down?

Assuming that in-store sales are their key measurement, then they are, according to Charles Herrick with whom I simply won't argue, in the meeting-place business! Do you see very many people sitting around by themselves? Even if they are sitting by themselves, they are on their laptop or texting back and forth with someone. They now need to drive a ton of energy into making Starbucks a <u>desired</u> place to meet, not just a place to have a quick business meeting because you can't think of anyplace else.

So, if they are in the meeting business, is Starbucks a great place to meet? Well, where else are you going to go? The meeting industry has not caught up with the nation's transient, mobile workforce. I often think twice about going to a coffee shop for a meeting – not just Starbucks but any good coffee shop. I hate getting a table and then having two housewives park themselves and their strollers next to me then let their little snots cry.

---

[10] I'm not sure if they will still be playing it when this book comes out. They should do like everyone else is doing and play music from the 60's and early 70's. We all know that was the best era for music. Quick! Name 5 great songs from the last decade. And going back to the original topic, name 2 great jazz songs. Who was Miles Davis? Okay, you flunked. You don't like jazz either; so quit faking it. Back to Led Zeppelin and Three Dog Night...

When it's crowded I don't like going to Starbucks for a meeting but, as I say, where else am I going to go? It's noisy. Why don't they add white noise to drown out the other conversations?

If Starbucks decides they are in the business of making meetings a treat, they will come along strong. In the meantime, McDonalds is coming along with McCafe. Which place will offer the bigger treat? McDonald's is following behind Starbucks who essentially created the retail gourmet coffee industry. (I know Peet's and others were first but they didn't create the industry; Howard Schultz and Starbucks did). McDonald's is essentially entering the alternative-to-Starbucks-business. So if you decide you don't want to pay $3.50 at Starbucks for your double-tall vanilla latte, then you go to the drive-up window at McDonald's. Lattes are the fundamental beverage of the gourmet coffee world. I know. I ran that coffee roasting and retail company for three years. Maybe they should open up a business-version of Starbucks – Starbucks, Inc. Shops, with little meeting rooms, Wi-Fi, a wall full of docking stations, and gigantic speed bumps to keep out baby strollers, I say, misanthropically.

To succeed in their business, McDonald's needs to nail down making a good latte. And if they can do that *and* Starbucks doesn't become a better (more comfortable) place to meet, then they will either have to lower their prices and take a severe hit on margins or they will hit the wall hard and have a very tough time making it to the next level. Or the business they are in will change and they'll adapt. But then it seems like it will require Schultz to remain perpetually in the CEO position.

Oh, and one other thing for coffee shop owners. How about putting up some clocks on the walls so that those of us who are meeting don't have to keep peeking at our watches and cell phones? (Author's note: When you sneak a peek at your watch or cell phone, everyone knows it. It's hard to be considered polite when you're being coy. Who do you like better – the guy fakes a yawn and looks at his watch or the guy who says, "I need to be conscious of the time?").

You better know what business you're in. Take a minute or two to figure out what business you are really in. Then call me and tell me what it is. I'll tell you you're wrong. I'll make you feel pathetic and then you'll hire me. I'm in the sound-like-I'm-smart-and-I-have-all-the-answers business.

Let's look at another case history on the subject of knowing your business:

I was brought into STAR Consulting, a large systems integration firm, as the heir apparent to the CEO, who was one of five owners and founders. The company had approximately 700 employees with about 300 of them working in Seattle where headquarters was located. I was the new VP of the Seattle operation.

There were two other companies in town that were the same size. This was during the dotcom boom and they were our archrivals for a lot of high- tech integration business. Seattle was one of the three big centers for the high-tech industry, along with the Silicon Valley and Boston.

I sat down with the CEO and former owner on my third day. He was turning Seattle over to me after managing it directly himself for the last several years. He pulled out a big stack of papers, each with a little yellow sticky note attached and then he started taking me through them. The conversation went something like this:

Lloyd: Okay, so here's the list of what we spent in the lunchroom last month. You'll see that napkin usage is suspiciously high.

(He hands me the paper. I take it but I don't look at it).

Lloyd (continues): And here are the names of the data base administrators who started on the project at AT&T.

(He hands me the paper. I take it but I don't look at it).

Lloyd (continues): And here is the invoice for the new laptop one of the testers just ordered. I frankly think he loaded it with features he didn't need.

(He hands me the paper. I don't even take it. Instead I put my hand on the stack of papers).

Charles: Lloyd, Lloyd, hold on a second. I'm sure there's lots of good stuff in that big ol' stack of papers. But before we get going, let me just ask you this: It took you four months to recruit me. I was kind of a pain, I realize that. But when you hired me and I signed the employment contract, what were you thinking on your way home? When you thought to yourself, "Okay, I just hired Charles Herrick and now he's going to…" (I looked at Lloyd to fill in the blank).

Lloyd: I don't understand what you're asking.

Charles: When you got me to sign up and you were thinking how good it was going to be to have me on board, what were you hoping I would accomplish. What *big* things - not count the paper towels; but things like increase market share by X amount, etc.

Lloyd: Well, we're growing at less than 10%…

Charles: The company is growing at 6% - and in Seattle it is growing 0%. I checked.

Lloyd: So, I guess I'd like to see that brought up to about 15 to 20%.

Charles: Okay, what else? Give me one more big one.

Lloyd: Well, people are a bit unhappy these days. They aren't getting to work until about 9 and they leave before 5. I'd like to see morale come up a bit.

Charles: The place is empty until about 9:30 and they've been leaving at 4. And they all hate each other.

Lloyd: Well, I'm not sure…

Charles: Okay, so grow 20% and get the people to have a little spring in their step. Got it. Anything else big – or will that do it?

I stood to leave. As I did, I put my hand back on the stack of papers and said, "You hang onto this here stack of papers. I'm sure I'll be back asking for something in there but I don't think I need it right now."

I started to walk out and then I sat back down. I had one more question. I asked him, "Lloyd, what business are we in? What would you say in a short phrase if someone said what do you do – what business is the company in?" The company did have the word "Consulting" in its title.

Lloyd responded by saying the obvious, "We're in the *consulting* business."

I just nodded and left to go turn things around. This was a crazy time in the industry. Everybody needed information technology developers and consultants but they couldn't find them. Companies like STAR had recruiting staffs constantly looking for these professionals so they could hire them and put them on projects for the client. STAR had 5 recruiters in Seattle.

It was so hard to get and keep good people that horror stories began to emerge about being held for ransom by people with even very weak skills. The worst I heard in that first week was the one about a consultant we had hired, taken through orientation and then sent out to the client's job site. He never made it. That afternoon the client

190

called us asking where he was. We tracked him down. On the way to the client's job site, he had gotten another call on his cell phone and was offered a job paying five thousand a year more. He drove over to the new opportunity and went to work there without ever telling us.

Despite the desperate battle for resources, Lloyd asked me a week later to lay off one of the five recruiters in order to save money. I refused. He was astonished that I would say no.

"Lloyd, I can't do that. That's the business we are in right now. We are all fighting for resources. We are in the recruiting and retention business. We need twice as many recruiters, better search software, a recruiting manager and faster process for getting them hired. We also need to do a better job of screening so I'm implementing a tech testing program that will replace the lame technical interviews we've been doing.

"Finally, I am changing the way sales works. Anyone can go to the client site and get a list of job openings and projects. What we need to do is hire commonly needed skills and then find the place to put them.

"Once we get our profits up, we will get out of that ugly business and then we'll move into specialties that we can own and dominate, similar to what we did at IBM. We'll take on huge projects, bid fixed price and build teams to deliver.

"So, no – I won't fire one of the recruiters because we will need lots more of them."

Eventually we put in place a number of programs designed to retain employees so we didn't have to recruit so many. It worked. Our turnover rate was exactly one third the industry average and only 30% of our two biggest rivals.

We grew 74% that year and I took over as the CEO.

By the way, life was a party at STAR. The air was electric and I often had people sitting in my office at 7 AM - something that never happened in Lloyd's day. Lloyd liked money – not people.

More later on the morale story.

So, what about the retention business? I took a huge risk when I changed our bench policy but I had to do it. The bench is a term used when someone comes off of a billable assignment, has no assignment to go to and yet you still have to pay them a salary. Hence, they sit on "the bench" until they are called back for an assignment. Lloyd had only allowed a small bench.

On my second week at STAR, I went into the kitchen to get some coffee. As I entered, a very polite Chinese woman got up from her stool at the counter against the wall and bowed to me, smiling. She was working on one of three back-level computers that were sitting on the counter facing a blank wall. This wasn't the bench. This was the Lubyanka. I wondered if they were delivered to the kitchen in a Black Maria.[11]

About an hour later I went into the kitchen and there she was again. She hopped up bowed and smiled. I nodded and smiled. She went back to work and I went back to my office.

When this happened a third time, I made a comment to my secretary about the fact that this thin Chinese woman must have a tapeworm because every time I went into the kitchen, she was in there, too.

"Oh, that's the bench," my secretary told me. "That's where people go when they come off assignment and we're still paying them. Lloyd allows up to three people on the bench at a time."

---

[11] The vans which the KGB used to pick up prisoners - 'черный ворон' or 'тюремная карета' to you purists.

"Out of 300 employees? He allows only 3?"

No wonder people were quitting. They knew that as soon as they came off of an assignment, they were likely going to be fired. So, rather than wait for that to happen, a month or two before their assignment ended, they started looking for another job. Sometimes they waited until the assignment was done; often they left just before it was done. This forced us to scramble and hire someone for as little as two weeks to finish the job. In the meantime, we lost another employee. In a roaring market, why would we do that? Instead, we needed to keep them, let them sit for a bit and then get them on another assignment.

With a more robust growth curve, we were in need of a better way to deal with people suddenly hitting the bench. I took one of my employees, and put him on a new assignment as the manager of the bench. His job was to coordinate between sales, recruiting and field projects managers to find jobs for people *before* they hit the bench. We called it the "Virtual Bench" – kind of a reverse war room. It worked. Roc was a fabulous bench manager. Whenever he would clear the bench, he would stop by and tell me had done so. When I asked him what he was going to do for a while, he would say, "I was thinkin' of beatin' your ass in basketball. " Roc managed the bench for a looooonnnnng time.

One other thing we did to reduce the recruiting load was to educate our software developers. If a person who was trained in Visual Basic (VB) was left on an assignment using VB 5, when the new version VB 6 came out, he would often quit and go someplace where he could keep his skills current. To solve that problem, I asked one of our recruiters, who was thinking of leaving the business, to take on a new assignment.

I found out that she had managed the internal education department at Nintendo. I asked her to start one at STAR. The only difference between what I wanted her to do versus what she had done at Nintendo was I wanted her to make them free classes internally but open them up to outsiders for a fee. She did a great job. The education department was hugely profitable and people kept their skills up without quitting.

So that's what you do when you know what business you're in. We added more people in one year than our two competitors combined added in two years. Our additional employee contingent was greater than the entire employee base of my competitors who had been the same size as STAR at the start of the year. It would have cost us $30 million to buy one of them. Instead, we just hired the equivalent and made a profit in the process.

Now that you know what business you're in, what are you going to do about it?

Chapter Ten

The Transmission of WHAT

And the Avoidance of Parallax

Those of us who have had multiple layers of management below us on the org chart have shared a similar musing: I wonder if the folks in the organizations reporting up to me are working toward what I'm working toward?

This is not something that only an executive or middle manager should be thinking about. It counts for the first level manager as well. But the more layers you have, the more critical it is that you have everyone lined up along the narrow path you're treading toward success.

If they aren't lined up, you have a situation I call parallax, which is a phenomenon that occurs when it merely looks like things are lined up. Here's the Merriam-Webster definition for those who really must know the etymology of my metaphor, which is more commonly used in the discussion of astronomy and telescopes:

Main Entry: **parallax**

Pronunciation: parˈⱥ ɪlaks

Function: Noun

The apparent displacement or the difference in apparent direction of an object as seen from two different points not on a straight line with the object.

I have no idea what that means.

However, here's what I̲ mean:

The mistaken belief that the goals and operations of departments within an organization are all lined up and aimed at the success of the organization overall, with each level in the hierarchy working to achieve the success of the level above.

In other words, if Fred reports to Susan and Susan reports to Tracy, parallax is occurring when Tracy asks this question:

If Fred is making his numbers and Susan is making hers, how can I be missing mine?

Or Tracy asks this question: Why am I now reporting to Susan?

An assumption was made that Susan was operating in Tracy's best interest. This is always a serious mistake. Susan was operating in Susan's best interest. Tracy feels betrayed because she had *faith* in Susan. Faith is noble. However, she didn't have faith; she had presumption. In business, you must have some degree of trust.

However, as my grandmother used to say:

Trust everyone...but cut the cards.

Here is a rule:

When it counts, employees will always place their own best interest in front of the best interests of the company or their manager.

Wake up! This is America. This is not Japan. In Japan you have a dozen people looking at you to make sure that what you do is directly beneficial to the company. You cannot get promoted unless what you do helps the company. There is also an attitude in the Japanese culture which places high value on doing what is right for the greater organization: home, village, country, company.

In America, the only time that happens is in a severe crisis such as in all-out war or a hurricane.

Salesmen have known this fact for years when selling high ticket items. People all along the decision chain make decisions and recommendations that protect their jobs. It was never more apparent to me than when I was selling multi-million dollar mainframes.

Here's the story.

At that time, a corporation as large as Safeco often had their entire company running on one computer. If the computer went down, thousands of people could be idled, customer satisfaction could fall apart and morale could plummet. It cost a fortune to be out for a day.

I can remember standing in the huge computer room at Safeco surrounded by hundreds of machines on standby, waiting for the Field Engineers to get the giant, multimillion dollar mainframe running again. This was a rare occurrence. Standing next to me was the president of the company, the VP of Administration and the VP of MIS along with all the data processing operations managers.

One of the Safeco managers and I had become good friends. He turned to me and asked quietly, "How long before it's fixed?" I turned to him and asked quietly, "How long does it take to catch a fish?" We both suppressed a laugh. Gallows humor.

The president looked my direction and asked me the same question. I was the IBMer responsible for the data center representing 95% of IBM's business at Safeco – a lot of responsibility for a 26 year old kid. We were standing amid approximately 100 million dollars' worth of IBM equipment and I had an immediate backlog of equipment I was trying to sell that totaled about $15 million. I needed a slightly less clever answer than the one about how long it takes to catch a fish.

I couldn't think of one.

The Field Engineer heard the question and caught my eye. He shook his head subtly, trying to let me know it didn't look good. I gave the best answer I could. Sobriety set in.

"It could take long enough that we will have to go through the recovery/reprioritization process that your folks have in place. I've asked two systems engineers who specialize in that to leave what they're doing and help out. When the system comes back up, we'll do everything possible to catch up quickly."

I had called the systems engineers almost immediately after I heard the mainframe had gone down. It was an honest answer – the best answer. This was deadly stuff for the careers of all kinds of people. It would factor into future actions and future procedures. I had to make sure that the decision was never in doubt as to why on earth they had chosen the IBM machine.

Gene Amdahl, founder of Amdahl Corporation, our biggest competitor, felt that we took unfair advantage of the tendency for people to do what was right for their careers and not what was right for the company. He said we sold the FUD factor: Fear, Uncertainty and Doubt. Here's how it works:

In those days, the likelihood that a mainframe would go down sometime during the year was about 99%. You therefore had to bet that it would go down at least once and probably more than once. One of those outages could be prolonged. If the system went down hard, and you were the guy that made the decision for the Amdahl, how many people would be wondering if you had done the right thing buying *that* instead of the IBM computer? The answer: Everyone, including yourself, despite the fact that the air-cooled Amdahl had a superb record of reliability, they always had an engineer onsite, and the machine was often priced $2 million lower than the equivalent capacity IBM mainframe. In making the Amdahl decision, you were ostensibly saving the company $2 million dollars for the same processing power.

Unfortunately, saving money gets you a one-time pat on the back – unless your boss takes credit for it. If that happens, you don't really get a pat on the back. Remember, those decisions were reviewed all the way up the chain. It is much more likely that you will get lasting credit for the big mainframe that now has pneumonia than you will be remembered for saving money with the lower-priced Brand X.

On the other hand, if you had picked the IBM mainframe, you were not going to be asked why you hadn't gone with the machine that was chosen 98% of the time. So, if you can justify the price difference (and we supplied you with everything you needed to do that) then you were a lot safer going with IBM.

My next job after handling the Safeco account was to go to San Francisco for the most prestigious staff job you could get at my level. In those days you went field to staff to field to staff until you were really high up. (I viewed the higher ups as staff, by the way).

My job was to come in during a competitive battle and convince the customer that our $4.1 million dollar 3081 was less expensive than an equally powerful, very reliable, used Amdahl V8 priced at $800 thousand. It was going to be a while before Amdahl came out with their new series and they were having a fire sale to hold the line.

My predecessor in the job had lost 27 times the year before and had already lost 4 times by March of the year I took over from him. Despite the losses, he got promoted because we were in the backyard of our two biggest competitors – Amdahl and NAS, both built primarily on Japanese technology. At 27 losses, our West Coast region had the worst record in the country. I had the rest of the year to figure out how to beat a good machine that was priced 80% lower than ours.

I soon found out why we lost. When I went through the transition with my predecessor, he showed me all the presentations he had done, proving how our operating systems ran much better on our machines. The Amdahl computer was IBM-compatible but it didn't have the same amount of microcode hardwired into the computer to speed processing. He had a presentation for both MVS-XA and VM our two big operating systems. He made these presentations all the way up to the Board in some companies.

At 8 PM he left me to my thoughts as I looked through the big presentation notebooks. When I heard the elevator ding to take him down to Market Street, I waited 20 seconds and then tossed the notebooks in the trash. I was *never* going to show them to *any* executive. Who cares about microcode at that level? True, I needed to be prepared to answer the question as to why ours was better; however, the guy who made the decision was not going to be the third shift operations manager who oversaw the nightly batch runs. The guy who made the decision was always a higher level executive – and his career was potentially going to be affected by what he chose. There was only neutral or *downside* potential for him in making this decision.

My job on the other hand was to make sure he looked good when he went forward with his decision. I did this by capitalizing on past failures. Each time a computer was bought, it was forecasted to last for 5 years. Typically, it lasted two years, sometimes two and a half. A big company had hundreds of application programmers writing code. Where do you think that code was going to run – on an abacus? It always took more code and was used more heavily than anyone had expected. In the meantime, people at their desks were expecting faster and faster response time, which required a faster computer, which got more people on at once, which drove up utilization, requiring a new computer way sooner. I should have called the Federal Reserve and confessed that we were opening up our own mint.

Since our 3081 system was at the beginning of the product line and therefore upgradable, I could make the case that they would have to expense the Amdahl over two years and ours could be cost out over five years because the underlying machine would still be there when it was upgraded. Amdahl's counter was: Buy the Amdahl V-8 now and wait for Amdahl's next computer. If you don't like what you see, install the IBM system in two years; then merely add the price of their computer to the price of the IBM computer and expense it over 7 years.

I wasn't done yet.

When you added up all the extra costs such as maintenance (lower with ours and free for the first year), then put in the tax effect of Reagan's ACRS (accelerated cost recovery system), you had a much narrower price gap because you couldn't depreciate a used machine as fast as you depreciated a new one. "In two years, what was a used Amdahl going to be worth?" I asked. Whatever they spent on the Amdahl was simply an extra expense because it was going to be tossed out at the end of two years, unsalable. And they would still have to buy a new computer – likely mine.

I was going to make sure that my case was heard at all levels. The savings with the competition was now very questionable. Still, it could be argued that you might save a couple million dollars.

So, Mr. Executive, what's in your personal best interest?

I only lost three times and I never mentioned XA or VM, which were important technical considerations but they would not affect someone's career. *But having a computer crash when I had muddied up the waters so much on the finances would affect someone's career!*

So what's this got to do with parallax?

What if the CEO were to overrun his expense or capital budget later that year? Every major expense item would be scrutinized. The computer decision would come up and one of his detractors would then be able to do his own water-muddying. Do you think the CEO would care about the fact that the VP who made the computer decision was safe in his job? It was probably still the right decision and the CEO could probably still make his case, but don't we have parallax? The VP was making a decision based on what he would look like if the computer went down; the CEO was interested in the P&L. It could be argued that they are actually well-aligned. But if they are, it is only by coincidence.

If parallax could occur to the tune of millions of dollars on a very visible decision, how often does it occur in less definable actions? The real question should be: How do you make sure it doesn't happen?

What do you need to do to ensure that when your people succeed at their objectives, you succeed at yours?

It's real simple:

Keep your organization flat, your objectives few, and your measurements accurate and relevant.

To expand on my grandmother's aphorism: Trust everybody but play with only a couple of people you can beat up if they cheat, play a game you know very well, and wear your eyeglasses when you cut the cards.

How does this work? Let's look at another STAR Consulting example.

Just before I became CEO, the former CEO, Lloyd, brought in his old buddy Mel to run the Albuquerque office and manage some of our West Coast branches, including Los Angeles and San Diego.

Mel was from a world much different from IBM. He was what most people would call a loveable slob. We had some things in common: I deplored sloppy execution and so did he. He deplored sloppy execution because he loved *really* sloppy execution. I stayed away from cigarettes; he kept them exactly a full arm's length away, (when exhaling). I have a 29 inch waist; he has two 29 inch waists. We were like twins – or maybe triplets. However, our financial performance results made us look like one of us (I vote for him) came from a planet in another solar system. I'm thinking it was one of those planets where if you forget to water your parched plants for a year, they grow anyway.

When I took over as CEO, believe it or not, I did not try to change his sense of commercial horticulture. I just wanted him to change his results and I wanted him working toward some very ambitious goals. By now I had brought in a new VP for the northern offices and some other solid IBM-types. Mel was now playing on a team of starched-collar professionals.

I explained that I wanted to make sure they had as their top priorities initiatives that lined up with my priorities. They needed to be written down. They also needed to ask the same of their immediate subordinate managers, who in turn...

Mel didn't take this too seriously. When I asked him to tell me what his initiatives were, he started in on a list of things he was working on. I stopped him on about item 8. I asked him for his secretary's phone number. I told him if I wanted his to-do list, I would call *her*. I wanted to know what one or two things he was going to do to make me rich. If I had asked him what he was going to do to make the company better or help hit our quarterly targets, he would have gone back to his to-do list, explaining how each of those would help move us along. Instead, I came up with a slightly corny term called a *two*-do list. It could have one or two items at the most on it which, when executed, would make me rich. I would be the judge, basing my assessment almost entirely on the size of my bank deposits - not really how I think but it was a good way to make a point.

Over the next couple of months he caught on and actually was very good at knowing exactly what big things to be working on. He also required the same of his direct reports. I didn't need to run planning sessions; I knew exactly what the output of their individual planning was. People know what to do. You sometimes just have to force them to clarify their intentions. Otherwise, how do their people even know what to do? And how do I know that what everyone is doing will actually help me achieve the company goals?

The next step was building a new reporting system. The former CEO had an endless list of things he followed.

Here's a rule that you didn't need to buy this book to learn:
When you emphasize everything, you emphasize nothing.

If you emphasize every measurement, over time you create a pattern of what you are interested in and people begin letting certain things drop through the cracks, assuming you won't ask. Is that how you want people to figure out your priorities?

One of the best movies ever on bad management is the 1999 flick *Office Space*. Toward the end, this poorly run hi-tech firm brings in the consultants. They gather everyone together for a standup meeting and display a banner which reminded everyone to constantly ask themselves: *"Is This Good for the Company?"* It's a pretty obnoxious way to get already dispirited employees to help move the company forward. However, among the management crowd, each level has to answer the question on that banner and define its own initiatives accordingly. If you, as the upper-level manager, have to constantly make sure the actions of your subordinate managers are in line with your goals, you are doing their jobs for them. If their initiatives don't line up with the top guy's, it's not going to work. The top guy needs to have measurements that tell him either he is going to make it or he is not going to make it.

In today's data rich, real-time world, waiting until the end of the month, quarter, or year to find out if you made your numbers is unconscionable. Therefore, it starts with an early assessment of alignment vs. parallax and it continues with an ongoing look at results to date and what's being done to ensure hitting the target.

> Here's another key rule:
> **What gets measured gets managed.**

> Here's one more:
> **Management is 80% follow-up.**

> A corollary to that is the old trite saying:
> **Don't expect what you don't inspect.**

People will focus on just about anything that gets put on a report, if there aren't too many things being measured and "emphasized."

If you have only three measurements that you post in the lunchroom each week, and one of them is a measure of how many paper towels each person uses in the bathroom, I can guarantee you the number of paper towels used will plummet. Make it so that each time someone wants a paper towel in the bathroom, they have to swipe their employee ID barcode through a little slot on the dispenser. Your present stock of paper towels will last two years.

You could also possibly keep people working at their desks longer and save on your water bill if you measured...

It's fine to measure lots of things. Sales departments routinely use CRM software to track leads. When did the lead come in? How long before it was followed by action? What came of that action? How many leads resulted in what number of sales?

What you start with is a basic understanding of what it will take to make the numbers. The IBM typewriter and copier guys (amazing salesmen) had a rule: Calls plus demos equals sales. If their sales fell off, they looked deeper and sometimes really delved into the details. But for the most part, they tracked the number of in-person calls, how many of those calls led to demos, and how many demos led to sales.

They kept it simple from an emphasis standpoint but were prepared to go into deep detail if necessary.

Here's another way to look at setting objectives and keeping it simple. Just as in the example I'm using, it takes some work to figure out, but once you do, it pays huge dividends.

I once came home early and went into my backyard to relax. Up the way, sitting on his back porch was Nick Kirschbaum. He was a rocket specialist. He was having a beer and celebrating all by himself. I asked him what he was celebrating.

Nick:	We had a successful rocket launch today.
Charles:	What did you do?
Nick:	We shot a small rocket from our airbase here and it hit within a hundred feet of its target.
Charles:	Where was the target?
Nick:	Floating in the Atlantic Ocean
Charles;	So, the rocket must have had a good guidance system.
Nick:	Nope. Just a regular rocket with regular fuel.
Charles:	Then how could you get so close, three thousand miles away?

206

Nick: Four thousand. All you have to do is have the right amount of fuel and hit two small, imaginary hoops up in the sky. If it makes it through one hoop and then the other, it has to land where you want it when it runs out of fuel. You just do the math, determine the hoops, aim the rocket and press the button. It took us a while to figure out how to aim the rocket but now we have it pretty solid. With a handful of rockets, we can take out a large ship within 5 or 6 thousand miles, no sweat.

The IBM Office Product guys selling typewriters and copiers knew their two hoops. If ten sales calls led to one demo and five demos led to one sale, then you needed fifty calls to get five orders. Of course, it got more sophisticated based on the type of territory. But that was just an adjustment in the hoops. Maybe it took 500 calls in downtown Newark office buildings. So how many do you want to sell? Then make X number of calls and Y number of demos.

Everything starts with sales. If you're thinking that I earlier used an example where everything started with recruiting during the dotcom boom, you're right. But they are not mutually exclusive. In a highly competitive marketplace, recruiting *is* sales. We were selling prospective employees on why they should work for us instead of the ten other companies that wanted to hire them. We knew our productivity per recruiter. We knew how many people turned over each month. We knew how many people we wanted added to do billable work. We knew how many people each salesperson could place. We knew how many big projects were in the pipeline and which project sales lead or project manager was driving the big deals.

I knew this because I asked for it via summary roll-up. My direct reporting executives also knew it. We therefore managed the number of recruiters and sales people, aimed them at the right set of clients and the results poured in. In the meantime, we did all the necessary things to increase productivity, reduce turnover, improve customer satisfaction and follow-up, reduce expenses, etc. But we had already turned the large dials.

We emphasized the big things, managed them closely and then did our daily jobs as managers.

This works for accounts receivable departments, putty knife assembly lines, you name it. Find out what two or three things have to happen to give you your results and then drive a ton of energy in that direction. Then fix problems, improve processes and tidy up.

We talked about people management earlier. But this is what you do to win, department by department. As an executive or manager, you just need to be sure that you know the hoops and everyone else knows them, too.

Got time for one more?

If you're wondering about the accounts receivable department example, I'll toss this in as a bonus. Days Sales Outstanding (DSO) is the primary measurement of a company's overall AR collection effectiveness. Simplistically, if you sell or perform 100,000 dollars' worth of business on average each day, and your present accounts receivable totals $6 million, then your DSO is 60.[12] That's a little above the acceptable average in the consulting business. In the Seattle office, ours was about half that, which sounds impossible but it's true. Here's how we did it.

In the past, when an invoice was approaching 90 days old, the AR department would start to plead with the salesperson to go collect it. The salesperson had already been paid and he wanted to do more

---

[12] I know the real way to do it is with Total Credit Sales, etc. It's boring. Okay?

business with the client; so the last thing he or she was going to do was go make an embarrassing call on the client and call him a deadbeat.

But I saw it differently. The AR clerk had no clout. I was paying the salesperson on the basis that the company was going to get paid. If that wasn't going to happen, then I wasn't going to pay the salesperson. So we put in place DSO measurements by territory. If you had a DSO of more than 50 days, then you had to present your plan to fix it. If you had an invoice older than 60 days, that invoice amount would be deducted from your next commission calculation, it would go back in at 50% of value, once you did collect it. If you got your DSO under 40 and no invoices over 60, you got a bonus. If it's important enough for me to whine about, I ought to be willing to pay a little extra if it goes equally far to the good. The salesman needs to keep the client from *becoming* a deadbeat.

The guy that ran the huge Boeing account came to us and cut a deal. If he could get his DSO under 35 would we be willing to give him a very large bonus? Since the Board was measuring me on DSO, I of course agreed. The reason I did so was because Boeing represented 20% of my Seattle business. I gave him the go ahead, knowing he had something up his sleeve already. He had worked out a direct wire transfer for any invoice that was signed off on by a Boeing manager. Since he always knew what the billing was going to be by Friday morning, he just had the invoices printed off and got them signed. He then walked them to the AP department at Boing and they were paid on the following Monday.

So what were our two hoops to achieve a low company accounts receivable DSO? Territory DSO and invoices older than 60 days. The commission plan and incentive plan, along with standard "coaching," took care of the rest from a management standpoint. Easy stuff.

What about the first rule in avoiding parallax – keeping your organization flat?

Most organizations have too many managers. Each manager has too small a span of control, i.e., he or she isn't managing enough people. Here are possible reasons why:

- Upper management is lazy
- Upper management is incompetent
- Upper management is cowardly

Figuring out how to organize is hard work. What are your critical functions and who should run them? An alternative to figuring this out is to just create little bunches of people and give 'em a boss. Then demand all kinds of things from the boss until he can't deliver. Then you fire him/her. Hopefully (and likely) your competition is doing the same. Now make sure your desk is clean and go home and talk down to your wife. You'll feel like a tough guy.

If you don't know how to bunch people up in some quasi-logical fashion, then at least create organizations that *sound* good. Pull everyone into a room, announce your new organizational strategy, look about the room with a steely eye, saying tough-guy things. My favorites are:

"Okay, people, lock and load." Say this even though you used to wet your pants walking past the selective service office or whenever you watched a John Wayne movie.

Or you can say "This is where the rubber meets the road." Most people have no idea how that phrase came into common usage. But it sounds good. The only question is this: Are people going to do anything different because you said that?

"Today is the first day of the rest of your life." I feel better now. You just crammed your entire persona into a yellow smiley face.

In the meantime, you have made every third person a manager, so now anyone who is not a manager feels like he's done something wrong. You just played duck-duck-goose and created a management team.

Don't get me started. I've had to clean up hierarchical rats nests like this before.

This leaves us with the cowardly executive who has too many managers. Why is that? One reason is because he wants to reward good performers with a promotion rather than look those good performers in the eye and say, "Look, Karen, there aren't any management openings right now. Just keep doing what you're doing and I'll make sure you have a shot at a management role when one comes up. In the meantime, I'll see to it that your compensation matches your terrific performance."

Another reason is that it's scary managing certain people. If you don't fully understand your business and you have people that do, then get someone in between you and the smart guys. This often happens when someone from sales is put in charge of an operation that includes engineers or technical people.

Here's a rule for everyone, even if you plan to continue being a lousy manager:

Never create a funnel org chart.

A funnel org chart is where you have just one person reporting to you and then a whole bunch of people reporting to that one person. On a chart it looks like a funnel. Sooner or later, one of two things will happen: Your boss will realize that one of you is not necessary. The other thing that will happen is that your people will realize that *you* are not necessary.

Pare down your management staff. It requires much better managers to manage a large group but find those people and give them an organization. Don't create middle management positions that aren't needed and which just cause resentment and confusion. If one of your present managers isn't leading effectively, then take him/her out of management. You will boost morale sky-high and clear the way for sudden performance surges. People don't want to perform well for a jerk. But they will work around the clock for a real leader. That's the way we humans are programmed.

Here's a general formula:

If your managers focus on WHAT instead of HOW, you will need half as many managers.

It will save the company a lot of money in management salaries if the people in charge deal in business issues instead of personalities, and they deal in what needs to get done instead of the details of the approach the employees use to hit their targets.

One of IBM's seven principles was this: Managers will lead effectively. Lead is the key word here.

When I was at the bottom tier in IBM, I reported up through a marketing manager, branch manager, regional manager, division VP, division President, and then the CEO. IBM had 400,000 employees. I had five layers between me and the CEO. I know companies of less than 500 people who have more than 5 layers.

Take a look at your structure. If it's loaded with managers, suck it up and fix it. Communication in both directions will move more quickly and with a lot less need for translation.

BONUS INSERT
Prioritization

Since I mentioned "two-do" lists and my executives only giving me their top initiatives (ones that would make me rich), let me help with the other things you have to do as a manager. I don't mean to say there isn't a lot of housekeeping you need to take care of. I mostly mean that as your boss, I generally don't want to hear about it unless you really need my help. On your end of things, you do need to prioritize what you tackle every single day.

Prioritization, done only by itself, is a good way for indecisive, gutless managers to make themselves feel like they have a lot of work they need to get done and that it's all valuable. Otherwise, it wouldn't be in writing on a bona fide to-do list. Let me save you some time.

Efficiency experts, who are kind of icky people generally, will give you little tips such as "Make a list of all your to-dos; divide them into A, B, and C priorities; then turn each B into either an A or a C and voila! You have your day or week all laid out for you."

This may be good for entry-level clerks, but I kind of doubt it. What I don't doubt is that it is absolutely inappropriate for executives to set their agendas this way. It leaves out the most critical initial task, once you know your top one or two initiatives. What is that critical task? A process called: POSTERIORIZATION

Here's how it works.

Take your list of the 50 things you could be working on, generally sort out the lower 40 items, ask yourself if the world will end or babies will die if you don't do them, and then toss them out. If you make a mistake and toss out the wrong one, it will find its way back to you like one of those dogs in the movies that falls out of the car in Montreal

213

and somehow finds his distraught family years later in San Diego after fighting wolves and saving little girls from going over Niagara Falls.

"Oh look, honey, Snuggies found us."

"Alice, I thought you said leaving him at that gas station in Montreal would work!"

Snuggies (or your to-do) may come back feral and flea-ridden but he/it *will* come back – or find a new home, which is okay, too. You can deal with a to-do that reappears on your doorstep a lot easier than you can deal with doing everything on your original, exhaustive list. As you're going through your list, here's the little conversation you'll have with yourself when you're just learning the posteriorization game:

You: I *might* have time for that.
Smarter You: Nah.

[Cultural Note: The "a" in "nah" is pronounced like the "a" in apple. It sounds more decisive than "naw". People who say "naw" also say "Aw shucks." That's not very executive sounding.]

Posteriorization continues after you have gotten rid of the bottom 40, including your pet projects – your administrative version of Snuggies. Now take the ten remaining tasks and ask if it is something that it would be appropriate for someone else to do. Get rid of that one, too. Now you should be down to things that relate directly and obviously to your top one or two initiatives that will make me rich.

In general business, those to-dos should be directly related to sales, customer satisfaction, or stockholder value, to the extent that you, given your level in the management hierarchy, can influence. This is your litmus test.

This also means you need to apply the litmus test to all those reports you fill out all the time. Do they really meet the "two-hoops" test? Are they really going to land that rocket near the target? If not, it's time to talk to your boss and get rid of that report. In today's world of online everything, sales force automation, etc., reports should be produced by your business intelligence system, complete with dashboards and the ability for you *or your boss* to drill down.

Here's the rule in a well-run company:

The only work you should do on a report is analyzing and explaining results – not recording them.

Chapter Eleven
Decision Making and Execution

Here's how most people believe you make a decision:

You get all the data you can and then you start weighing the pros and cons of each alternative. Then the one with the most plusses gets chosen over the ones that don't have as many plusses or you choose the ones whose plusses are greater than the negatives.

Actually, this is how computers sort things - old-style computers.

Okay, so that's not such a good system – even though 70% of the managers I have known use something like it.

Here's a better one (sort of):

Do a yield-projection analysis. Add up the potential benefit of each element of your options, multiply them by the odds of them happening and then pick the one that adds up to provide you with the greatest yield.

Actually, this is how low-level accountants work. They get these assignments when the guys who are supposed to be making decisions chicken out and want documentation set up because they don't know what to do and it might fail and they want to point at the numbers and say, "Arthur in accounting gave me this list." That was a run-on sentence but I wanted to reflect the spirit of the process.

You're not an accountant. You're an executive. You don't add stuff up and then make a decision.

You make a decision by verifying your *sense* of what to do. If you're a good executive, then your gut feel will be right a majority of the time.

Here's the Rule:

Decisions are made by verifying a gut feel.

This is actually the second step in the decision process. Figuring out which problem to solve is the first.

Here's the rule:

Managers and executives make bad decisions because they are solving the wrong problems.

Not a single one of the managers that have reported to me has been stupid, inexperienced, or ignorant. Yet a number of them have made terrible decisions or have come into my office and presented absolutely awful recommendations. I would be sitting there, going through page after page leading up to the recommendation for a major action, hoping that we weren't headed where I thought we were headed. I then had to find a euphemistic way of asking, "What *is* this massive collection of pond scum?"

Always ask him or her (and yourself), "What problem are you trying to solve?" Then, as the person's boss, ask yourself, "Does this solve any of *my* problems?" Another question you can ask when someone brings you a fairly minor issue: "Why are you seeking *my* approval? Why don't *you* just do it?" (Answer: They want you on board if the thing blows up. On big decisions, I want to be apprised. On little stuff, I want your secretary to be apprised).

Are you running out of questions? I've got more.

"So, if you implement this program, how will you measure its success? How will it help you make your overall measurements? How will you know for sure that your new program has actually contributed and made a difference?"

The answer to the last question will get you a lot closer to what problem the manager is hoping to solve with his or her recommendation. It answers the question: What will change as a result of doing this? That begs the question: Why does it need to change?

This then takes you to the heart of the matter: It needs to change because _____ (insert problem here).

When you get a lot of stumbling and dissembling as an answer to the final question, then you know he or she is either: a) embarrassed with the solution; b) not prepared with all the facts; or c) (and this is the big one) they don't *want* you to know what the real problem is.

Another rule:

When a manager is solving the wrong problem, 80% of the time it is because they are solving a personal problem.

I said a "personal" problem – not a personnel problem. They are covering it up with a business maneuver or they are dodging a bullet that they think is going to get them demoted or fired, stagnate their career, lower their appraisal, or just plain embarrass them.

Here's how it works. With the names changed so I don't get too angry reliving it, the following actually took place. This is a conversation between a middle-manager and me:

Fred: I need to reorganize my department.

Charles: How come? (*I cleverly get right to the heart of the matter*)

Fred: I need to focus more on growing some of my second-tier accounts.

Charles: But 80% of your business is coming from the Edison account and that company is growing like a weed. They need tons of our services. What's this second-tier stuff?

Fred: But now that I've got that account under control, I want to start hitting the other accounts harder.

Charles:	Hmmmmmm. *(That's a sound I make when I'm suspicious)*
Fred:	So, I want to take Mary off of Edison and put her on three of these smaller accounts.
Charles:	But Mary's the best salesperson you have and the client loves her. She was next in line to take over Edison as the lead rep when Henry leaves. What will you do to replace Mary on the Edison account?
Fred:	I want to leave that up to Jason. I think I should move Edison over to Jason's department. It's a better fit. And then I could focus on my other accounts. I know it's a bit of a sacrifice in terms of prestige, but since I'm paid on percentage of quota, I'll be okay, once we make the adjustments for the individual account targets, of course.
Charles:	You never mentioned this before today. We met last week and you gave me no indication that you were planning to do something this major.
Fred:	Well, I wanted to have it all worked out before I proposed it to you. I've been giving it a lot of thought.

Here's a hint, if you're pretty sure humans are involved:

No one selflessly gives up a major account or a terrific employee for the greater good. They will sometimes give up a great employee to promote him or her but will often do so only if they think they can't get away with *not* promoting him or her. They will *never* give up a cash-cow account, unless things are really bad.

Let's continue with this conversation that's about ready to mousetrap on ol' Fred:

Charles: Here's the good news, I've given it plenty of thought.

Fred: Really? (*Fidgets.*)

Charles: How are things going on the Edison account?

Fred: Oh, you know, they're moving along. There are some challenges, but over time…

Charles: How about we go call on the Exec VP. I haven't talked to her in four or five months and I'd just like to get a sense as to how receptive she would be to any changes.

Fred: I suppose we could…I mean, if you really…

By now it should be clear that Fred was not reorganizing in order to refocus. He had a bad situation going on at Edison and he thought he could jump out of the way early enough to escape the fire and avoid detection. In truth, Jason would have been a better choice to manage it and eventually did get the account. But it was after a horrendous year where we lost a third of our consultants at one point, due to a variety of reasons that could have been prevented if Fred had come forward early enough.

Here's a more or less dependable statement:

You rarely get in trouble asking for help – especially if you do it before the body you are wheeling in to be resuscitated is cold and blue.

Later, we had the beginnings of a similar situation at Acme Wireless. Managers were starting to look around for other accounts. We had over 100 people billing on various projects. At an average of $125 per hour, we were generating over $12,500 per hour. That's $25 million per year.

We had a couple of major successes. One of the Big 5 Consulting Firms was struggling with a project to create Acme's wireless messaging function. At a point where things were particularly bad, we swooped in like good little buzzards and took over the project. We nailed the delivery. As a result we got a couple more of the tougher (i.e., high bill-rate) projects. Life was good.

So, why were project managers and high-powered developers suddenly starting to look around? I didn't know they were. But the VP who reported to me knew and treated it like it was just one of those things.

And then I got the call.

Vick Dolman was the CIO at Acme Wireless. His secretary called my secretary and scheduled "a short review" at 4:15 on a Thursday. To my shame, I had never met him before, even though he had been there for at least three months. When I showed up I saw that things were running just a few minutes late. I was offered coffee about a half dozen times by the sweetest, most compassionate secretary in the world. She looked around and saw Dolman's door open. And then, with a most lugubrious look on her face, she told me it was... (insert funereal organ music)... "my time."

As I walked toward his office, the president of one of our competitors walked out angrily and didn't even look at me as he stomped by. I suddenly thought, "They're tossing out consulting companies." This was done now and then by the larger corporations. They would hang onto a few firms such as Andersen or Ernst and Young and maybe a couple of the lower-margin contractors like Volt but everyone else got the axe. My company was next.

I entered the spacious office with a sense of righteous indignation. Vick was sitting at his round table. I reached to shake his hand but he held up a handkerchief to let me know he had a bad cold. I told him no problem, and then I said that I saw he was running a bit behind so I would make this brief.

There was no way I was going to let him have the first substantive words. My pre-planned sales pitch was now an ad hoc survival pitch.

I went to his whiteboard and asked if I could erase what was up there. I then showed him that on our last big project where we replaced a Big Five firm, our fees were two-thirds of what theirs had been and we did it in two-thirds the time they had projected. Two- thirds times two-thirds equals four-ninths, which is less than half.

"I hadn't seen this before," Vick said, nasally. He was actually a very pleasant individual and very sharp.

"I guess what I'm asking, Vick, is a shot at some of the larger projects. Are you aware that I previously ran the consulting group here in the Northwest for IBM and that I have a number of those guys working for me now? Some of us, including myself, have run projects as large as $50 million in other lives." He was not aware of this, either.

We escaped execution.

In a way, we didn't deserve to escape. We (I or my VP) should have told our story earlier. One of the reasons we didn't was because the VP had made the determination that if he presented that kind of analysis, then it would give away our strategic advantage. Our competitors could match our offerings. This is very flawed logic. If it's an advantage and the customer isn't aware of it, how do you capitalize on it? Also, one half of the competitive advantage was the fact that we executed so quickly and so well. You don't just flip a lever and do that. Our competitors would have to match what we had already worked hard to do, which was hire great people. To do that, you have to be an attractive enough company to get those people to even interview. Our low-priced competitors were not going to be able to do that, and the Big 5 firms couldn't afford to hire and retain such personnel at the same cost we could. We had a unique advantage and we unwisely had hidden it under a barrel.

The Lesson: *By hiding our advantage, the VP was solving the wrong problem. He was trying to avoid detection by competition when he should have been trying to reinforce a strong impression with the client.*

What should that VP have realized when everyone was looking around for a new assignment? People don't give up a good account without a reason and consultants won't *leave* a good account without a reason. The managers who were finding homes for the people that were asking to come off the Acme account were also solving the wrong problem. They were trying to keep key people happy and billing when they should have been finding out why everyone suddenly wanted out. And then they should have worked on this very serious problem while escalating it up to my level.

Today's Understatement: Losing $25 M per year is something I eventually would have noticed.

It never hurts to ask what someone expects to see when they come forward with a solution or you see them making a big decision – or sometimes a little one.

Manager: I'm going to do such and such.

Charles: Sounds like quite an undertaking. How will you know when you've crossed the finish line? What will the new world look like when you do?

If you don't handle it this way, then *you* are solving the wrong problem. You are trying to be a good guy instead of a good executive.

We've already talked about trying to be popular. Here's a refresher on the subject: It doesn't work.

I don't want to spend a lot of time on decision making because once you know what business you are in, and once you have the right people doing the right things, and once you know for sure what problem you are solving, the rest is easy.

Here's the rule:

**You or your people will always figure out *how* to
do something, once everyone knows *what* to do.**

We know that a decision starts with a gut feel, and then the decision maker verifies it to some degree, depending on time available and how impactful the decision will be. There is however some difference between a decision and a choice. A choice is static: Alice and Arthur are the two best candidates for marketing manager. I choose Alice.

So, now what? Do you send her an email and she moves into her new office? Then do you send one to Arthur and he goes back to filling out his expense report?

A decision is a stream of choices, once the fundamental choice is made. How do you communicate it? Who's going to take the lead and when will they get it done? What will tell you it's on track? What will tell you that the wheels are coming off? Who is going to be affected by this decision? Will this create a mess?

Let's talk about messy decisions: Firing people, shutting down divisions, telling someone they aren't right for the job, cutting someone's budget, cancelling a popular program, firing your worst customers (highly recommended), etc. These kinds of decisions invoke some big questions:

Will babies die? Will the earth explode? If the answer to both of those questions is no, then make the decision. Do your best to mitigate the damage and fallout, but make the decision.

225

Here's the rule:

Make the decision and then clean up the mess.

Here's another rule:

It is better to make the decision, be wrong and correct it, than it is to prolong the process or make no decision at all.

If after you make the decision all the headlights are coming at you, then you're probably on the wrong side of the road and you better move over. You'll know this soon enough. What kills you is the slow damage that accumulates when a decision is delayed. It hurts morale and it damages your image. People don't think of you as pragmatic, they think of you as weak. Time runs out and your options dry up. Nasty problems are like bacteria: they can divide asexually – and their numbers keep growing!

If you continuously find yourself on the wrong side of the highway, you're probably not in the right job. Remember, the most likely reason for making a bad decision is solving the wrong problem. However, if you keep solving the wrong problem then your powers of discrimination are inadequate due to inexperience, emotional immaturity, lack of intelligence or lack of intuition and insight. You suck. Go do something else.

The reason a person is a manager is not because he or she is cut from finer cloth. They are managers because they have management skills and proclivities.

I think I am a much nicer person than many of the tattooed basketball stars that play for the NBA. I'm way smarter. My communication skills are superb (I don't say "You know" after every sentence). Why won't they at least give me a shot at playing for the Lakers? How about putting me in during the last quarter of some game when the Lakers are way ahead? I won't ball-hog. And I've got this little move I do where I kind of look one way and...

Okay, you're the manager because you have manager skills. Here's a question: Are you the person who should be making the decision on everything that happens in your department?

The answer is: Yes. Yes, if you are Leonardo da Vinci plus – and this is important – an egotistical, megalomaniac who wants to create a Zombie-like workforce that stares at the clock all day.

You need to let your people make decisions and then watch the outcome. This will give you surprisingly good results. When it doesn't work out, it results in the instantaneous growth of your people. They become exponentially better businesspeople if they have to live with their decisions.

At Safeco, when an executive made a major decision, a meeting was put on the calendar for one year out. On the day the decision was reviewed, it was determined whether or not it had been a good or bad move; whether the follow-on ramifications had been handled well, and so forth. It was serious, career impacting stuff. It's a good idea at the executive level – kinda goes with the territory – but it should be less ominous at lower levels in the corporation. If you can keep it impersonal, focusing on performance, then it will be a growth experience resulting in better business along the way.

And isn't that what decision making is all about?

An Editorial on Humans Making Decisions

On a couple of occasions, I have come to my office early in the morning, and one of my managers was waiting for me. He or she would have been up all night preparing their story on a decision gone badly. The question haunting the manager was: "What's Charles going to do?" They feared me doing something precipitous.

However, it never turned out that way. My question was almost always, "So, what are *you* going to do about it, if anything?" That's right – if *anything*.

Here's a rule for life as well as business:
Sometimes bad stuff just happens.

This idea that it happened on his or her watch can be taken too far. Bad stuff happens that no one could have anticipated other than retrospective fibbers. If you watch the news these days, you would think that earthquakes and hurricanes were caused by some greedy business guy trying to shave two cents off the cost of every widget.

And even if bad stuff happens because someone messed up, people need a few get-out-of-jail-free cards or they will quit making even moderately risky decisions. They will begin to feel awful about themselves and they will exude a lack of confidence which can essentially be the death of leadership.

It is more difficult to lead when you don't quite feel good about yourself. And whether it's something you're born with or not, it can be overcome and you need to get over it. You have to do for yourself what you must do for your employees: Look at your strengths and quit getting hung up on your flaws or weaknesses. Quit judging yourself. For the most part I have quit judging myself.

I was finding too much stuff wrong.

Chapter Twelve
Morale
(And the Only Two Levers You Can Pull)

There is nothing more satisfying as a manager than watching a group of people enjoying what they do. Perhaps the only thing more satisfying, is watching a group of people enjoying what they do, who previously were miserable. It's actually simple to explain. This will be a short chapter.

As we have already discussed, running for homecoming queen, being the cheerleader, etc., can only hurt. If you want morale to go up, there are two rules:

Morale Rule #1 of 2:

Morale will go up if the people think that the company is headed toward success.

Morale Rule #2 of 2:

Morale will go up if Morale Rule #1 is in place and the manager is performing the basic functions of good management: Communication, delegation and recognition.

Do you tell people what's going on? Do you let them own their area of activity (a key element of "what" management)? Do you let people know in a timely fashion that they've done a good job?

Leadership obviously helps, but some managers are better leaders than others. To supplement, think of management as a profession and managers as professionals. Major League baseball players, master bricklayers, and soldiers impress you by just how good they are at doing what they do. Because of training and experience, they are way better than people who show up and just start playing baseball or fighting battles. It doesn't matter how good an athlete you are, you are not going to do well against a pro. It doesn't matter how scrappy you are or what a great shot you are, do not come up against the U.S. Armed Forces unless you are really, really well trained and equipped. Athleticism and scrappiness help, but almost always, the gap is too huge between a pro and a gifted amateur. So be a pro.

About a half year after taking over at STAR, I got a visit from Dwayne, the Chairman of the Board. He was 6'4" and atrociously overbearing. Once, on one of my visits to company headquarters back East, he and I got into a heated argument in the board room, regarding company direction. I remember looking at his top execs. They were sitting bolt upright, staring straight ahead, avoiding any eye contact with either Dwayne or me. One was visibly trembling. Dwayne managed by fear.

Dwayne had bought the company 22 days after I signed on. The deal had been in negotiation for months but one of the things that was keeping it from closing was the fact that the owners of STAR were required to find someone who understood the IT consulting business and who could run a large company with several thousand people across multiple locations throughout the western United States. After almost five months of irreverent interviewing on my part, I reluctantly took the job. As I mentioned, morale was worse than awful. It was toxic. The company spirit had a thready pulse.

A number of the changes we made got things turned around and the company grew more in the first month than it had the entire prior year. In addition, I did a lot of MBWA (Management By Walking Around). Since Lloyd, the former CEO, had always been cloistered reading numbers and spreadsheets, people were not used to this. I was constantly trying to figure things out, so I asked a lot of questions. People felt engaged. On some of the bigger things, I took a number of their suggestions and really worked them through. Then I would either implement them or come back and tell them why I wasn't going to carry out their recommendation. People felt like adults. They suddenly felt like they were on the team. And then we started winning. How could morale help but go up?

I hired Patrick, a great branch manager, to handle Seattle. He sat in the office across from me in the glass-and-brass corridor known as executive row. I mentioned to him one day that it felt odd that no one ever stopped by and stuck their head in the door and said hello. I was a fairly affable guy, as were the other couple of execs in the corridor. In addition to that, people in the non-executive offices and cubicles would be able to get to the lobby, lunchroom, restrooms, and the front door a lot easier if they walked past the executive offices. It was a 15 foot-wide corridor. But nobody came through there. I wasn't used to such isolation. Then one day, Patrick discovered the reason. It wasn't isolation: it was an untoward *insulation*.

"Do you want to know why nobody walks by our offices?" he asked, shaking his head, snorting out a little laugh.

"I can't imagine."

"The former regime forbade them to do so. They had the personnel manager inform everyone that they were to take the long way out the side hallway and not 'bother' the executives."

I was shocked. And then I had one of my moments of twisted inspiration. "Here's what we'll do, Patrick. Let's have a printing company make some high quality coupons that say 'GOOD FOR A FREE, ONE-WAY WALK THROUGH EXECUTIVE ROW.'" Then when someone does something even moderately good like cleaning up his desk, we hand him one."

That did the trick. People began bragging about filling their stapler or sitting up straight. It became a contest to get the most passes. That only lasted a couple of days but the point was made. People started using the corridor and no one really abused my open door style. They knew I was busy and they wanted me to get my job done because it affected them.

Later, as our growth became explosive, we would hold a one-day seminar for the 15 or 20 new employees we were hiring every week or so. To kick off orientation day, we set up a couple of tables in the executive corridor at about 7:30 in the morning with muffins, pastries, fruit and coffee. Then we had a mini-party with all of us from the internal staff mixing with the new hires. It was a great way to introduce the new folks to the company.

And I always got there early to get the oversized blueberry muffins from Larry's market. Hey, I'm an egalitarian – not a saint. Anyway, back to the science of morale.

So, Chairman of the Board Dwayne, the fearmonger, came for a visit. He mentioned that the place was jumping and that the energy was palpable. He knew energy was good for business. I knew it, too. In fact, it's even good for humans. Pulling out his little notebook, he asked me what my morale *programs* had been.

"Morale *programs*?" I asked. "You mean like handing out suckers at the door when employees come to work? Or like taking them out to lunch a lot?" He nodded while making notes.

"Look, Dwayne," I explained politely. "Programs are fuses you light every once in a while. Morale only improves if the people feel like the company is going to succeed and if they are being managed appropriately. We're steering the ship. They want to know if it's going to make it safely to port. If they trust us to get there, morale goes up. If they don't and we treat 'em lousy along the way, morale goes down. There. No suckers. No lunches." Dwayne was still perplexed but somewhat relieved that he wouldn't have to take a hundred thousand people in the parent company out to lunch. And have you seen the price of suckers lately?

Here's my final but very important advice on the subject:

A key factor in influencing the level of morale is how hard you make it look. You can actually work harder than you should. This can raise issues of the sustainability of success. So relax. Be cool. Figuratively, lean against the wall and let that cigarette droop from your lower lip. Be Marlon Brando – don't be Don Knotts. Keep a smile on your face. If you're huffing and puffing now when just regular stuff is happening, what emotional shape are you going to be in when it really gets tough? I want Humphrey Bogart, not some guy gnawing his nails.

A good metaphor comes from the first time I went mountain biking:

I was in the Squaw Mountain area at a resort. As mentioned earlier, several of us had been nominated by various IBM executives for creativity during IBM's dark years in the early '90s. There were morning seminars and then we had the afternoons off. Two of us went to the bike shop, got a mountain bike and proceeded to walk several miles up a rocky mountain road to the top of a local peak. Neither of us had ever been mountain biking. We hopped on our bikes and headed down.

The terrain was very rough and we quickly felt every rock we hit, big or small. We were hanging on for dear life because there were no guard rails and a long way to fall if we went off the road. After a few minutes of this, we stopped. We couldn't imagine another three or four miles. But after a while we hopped on and started down again. I don't remember how it happened but at some point I didn't hold on quite as tight. The handlebars rattled back and forth a bit but it didn't really cause the bike to change direction. And it took all the pounding off of my elbows, wrists and shoulders. It was a lot of fun.

The next time we stopped, the other guy was even more miserable. I explained to him what I was doing and how terrific it was making the ride feel. He said he would give it a try but he really didn't attempt to relax his death grip on the handle bars.

So, there were the two of us, riding side by side on the same road, at the same time, on the same kind of bike. One of us was having fun; the other was just wishing it was over. When we finished and he groaningly got off his bike, he wondered aloud if he would ever be able to have kids. I said, "The name's Bond...James Bond. I like it shaken, not stirred.[13]"

Some people just can't be cool. They keep thinking that when everything settles down and the weather is nice and the money is coming in and the competition is weak and...and...and...then they'll be cool. But the time to be cool is when the rough stuff is happening. Everybody can be cool when your pockets are full of cash and life is perfect. It's when three guys step out of the alley and tell you they're gonna cut ya in half with a chainsaw that you kind of sniff out a laugh and say, "Oh, that ol' party trick?"

---

[13] To prove how cool it was when James Bond ordered a drink, note that the Sean Connery version of Bond said this in almost all of his movies, starting with Dr. No. Then, in 2006 Daniel Craig was asked which he preferred and he said he didn't give a damn if it was shaken or stirred. All things considered, which Bond is more cool, Sean Connery or Daniel Craig? I rest my case. If the Commies (or SMERSH) are coming, I want Sean Connery driving up to my porte-cochere in his Aston Martin – not Dan.

Here's the Rule:

When your employees see you sweat and fret, you become permanently uncool.

You've been tested. You've been stretched and they found a big ol' hole in your character. Character holes are generally assumed to be congenital and permanent. You can still manage professionally but you've lost a fair chunk of your leadership capital. And how are they going to get into port safely if there isn't a leader?

So anyway, "Here's looking at you, kid."

Okay, that's it. Go manage.

Afterward

Generation Y and the Millennial Challenge

We as executives and managers have never faced a challenge as perplexing and potentially consequential as what now confronts us with the advent of the Millennials; also known as Generation Y. There are many reasons it is a challenge but most of those reasons also applied to Gen X and to some extent to Baby Boomers. In both of these more familiar generations, the problem was not that we were dealing with an individual and therefore only an individual's behavior, we were dealing with a mindset and a culture. The same is true of Millennials.

What makes the Millennial challenge different comes in two parts. The first is that we are so far behind the power curve in addressing it. The statistics, surveys, and polling data are now reflecting such an ugly reality of disenfranchisement that the "establishment" generation is surprised to the point of disbelief. They go into denial: "There may be a lot of disaffected Millennials out there – but not in our company". They question not themselves and their lack of awareness but rather the surveyors and pollsters. "Who are these aliens that they've been studying?" they wonder. Perhaps the title of this book ought to be *"A Guide to Managing Earthlings and Millennials"*.

The second aspect, even more troubling than the first, is the fact there appears to have been a sea change in values and it kinda looks permanent. Millennials don't necessarily want the same things we want. How do you offer incentives to people who don't seek the same things you do? It's like trying to get your cat to do tricks by waving a stalk of celery in front of its nose.

We Baby Boomers were called the *Me Generation*. But we at least tried to hide our narcissism. Tests done on Boomers decades ago and now repeated on Millennials show a huge jump not only in self-centeredness but also in an artificial self-worth. If you have spent your whole life getting praise and even trophies just for showing up and being you, what is going to make your specialness stop just because the scenery changes and you're now at work instead of in the classroom? And if you have never really had to accept the consequences of bad behavior, what are you going to think of some guy who now wants to discipline you or even discuss your most recent screw-up? When the neighbor came to the door complaining that a child was rude, lewd, or malicious, who did the mother's anger get directed at? As a Boomer kid you were guilty. Didn't even need a trial. But now, as a Boomer parent, you have a neighbor who is imposing his values on your family and telling you that something you treasure, something that is clearly a reflection of you, is less than good. The neighbor is the bad guy. He is hurtful. He is a hater. You make that clear to your neighbor and you make that clear to your Gen Y child.

Perhaps there is a third aspect to this whole problem that is the source of all this. Could it be us? The answer to this question is clearly yes. Boomers reared this new generation and a combination of boomers and Gen-Xers are managing them at work. I can't offer any help for the first part – the child rearing; but I can offer a potential prescription for the management side of all this. And along with that, I can offer both hope and incentive. This is a curable problem. But it is not curable in the old school way that has worked for the last 10,000 generations. We can't just wait for the Millennials to get a little older and then they'll see the error of their ways. Mark Twain once commented that when he turned twenty one, his dad suddenly got a whole lot smarter. In a technology-based world where youth perpetually has the advantage in the new tools of commerce, holding out hope that someone will want to be just like the people that preceded them is not a good strategy. This is especially true if you are their boss and they simply don't like you. Gallup has surveyed this subject extensively. My own studies have shown that only about a quarter of employees are bought in, and the number one reason they don't like they're disaffected is because they can't stand their boss. Take a look at the Gallup site where they draw similar conclusions.

That's where good management comes in. And that's where the hope is. Because if every other company is dealing with almost 3 out of every 4 employees "not on the team," and your company can permanently flip that around, how much better will you be able to compete? How much better will you be able to manage through tough times or implement a bold new strategy that requires everyone rowing in unison and continuing to pull at the oar when they can't always see the destination? How much better will you be able to compete for precious resources in the labor market?

So let's take a quick look at the problem, see how big the gap is that we have to close, and then outline a simple set of steps that will allow you to take everything you've read in this book so far and apply it specifically to the Millennial challenge. After all, bad parenting, morality-neutral schools and their failed social engineering, along with our management got us into this problem. Only one of those levers is still available to pull at this point.

In a letter to my managers back in the late 90s, I told them, among many other things, not to threaten Gen-Xers because they would rather lose their job and sleep in their car than work for a jerk. This is not true of Millennials. They will just go back home to mom and dad, even if they are in their 30s. What would have shamed a Boomer, is now viewed as a smart move by a Millennial and his or her peers.

Millennials leave home later, get married later, have kids later (if at all), and pursue careers later. In fact, pursuing a career might be the wrong term. It's more like pursuing a variety of paths that result in enough income to fulfill immediate needs and wants. And what they want is not what we wanted.

When I made up my mind to go for it at IBM, I wanted to prove myself so I could get into management as quickly as possible and once there start competing for the top spots in the company. It was a long, demanding pursuit with a lot of setbacks and a lot of unpleasantness (like moving my family four times in five years) but I never lost sight of the goal. I was a salmon. Of course it's all upstream. That's how it works.

Take that same Charles in his Gen Y incarnation and ask him what he wants and he will more likely say he wants first and foremost to be able to work from home and work fewer hours. If you remind him that fewer hours will mean less pay, he'll say, "Okay, if that's the way you want to be."

So does that mean Millennials will settle for less? Not at all. According to a survey by UCLA's Higher Education Research Council, 81% of college freshman state that becoming wealthy was very important to them, which is twice as high as the students who took the survey 15 years earlier. They want all the toys we wanted, they just see them coming more osmotically than we did. Hard work is a much less preferred route. How much? Only 25% of Boomers were willing to admit they just didn't want to work hard versus 39% of Millennials.[14]

---

[14] These statistics are from Jean Twenge's excellent book on Millennials: *Generation Me, Why Today's Young Americans Are More Confident, Assertive, Entitled--and More Miserable than Ever Before*, published by Atria Books.

I have had people in their late 20s and early 30s say something like this out loud – while sober.

We have a beautiful home on a lake in the suburbs of Seattle. My kids are Millennials and we have lived in this same general area for almost 30 years. One of the great things about our family is that we have all remained friends; to the point where my children often use our place for parties with their friends. This has given me access to a fair amount of Millennial thinking and mindset. It has been remarked to me more than once by intelligent and well educated young people that they will likely never have some of the things I have. They have known me for most of their lives. They have seen me build 3000 square foot decks, add on rooms, and completely remodel my own homes. They know I have other property, including a house built in 1933 in the historic district of Issaquah, Washington that I remodeled myself, converting it from a disaster to a home ready for a magazine spread. I even sawed my own lumber for the board-and-bat siding and made posts from huge trees I felled on one of my other properties. Many have stayed at my waterfront pied-a-terre in the San Juans that we have turned into a mini-resort.

In getting there, I have traded up, land-swapped, fought city councils, lawyers, and environmental activists. All these things were just part of getting there. That's not how a lot of Millennials view it. They simply believe I worked too hard and if that's what it takes, they aren't going to have what I have. "I'm just not willing to work that hard, Charles," one of them said to me recently. He said it with a degree of pride. Not because he prides himself on laziness or lack of industry. He takes pride for knowing his limits and accepting them. The hard work barrier is not something he wishes to probe.

How does the country move forward on that kind of attitude? Sure there are still plenty of hard workers among the Millennials but when the number of hard workers gets cut in half and the trend is for worse yet, don't we lose our edge as a people? We are the third most populous nation on earth with almost a third of a billion people. Big numbers, along with the degree of freedom we have remaining, give us greater odds of producing the geniuses that invent things, cure cancer, and start great rock groups. But if the next generation of Steve Jobs and Jonas Salks prefers lip-synching and air-guitar to those long, hard, repetitive music lessons or their life-equivalents, then we are going to lose our technical, commercial, and cultural leadership unless the Gen Y bug bites India, China, and Korea as well. We are a big country that is about to act like a little country in net effect.

I attended Roosevelt High in Seattle. It was only a three-year school – no freshmen. We had a perennially strong football team because we had around 3,000 students to draw from. If someone had come along and said only people whose last names begin with the letters A through D can turn out, we would have been at the bottom of the standings because we wouldn't have that big pool of potential talent. That's the effect of enough people dropping out or saying they just don't want to work hard. Add to this the fact that men are dropping out in big numbers from applying for and attending college and you'll see we're walking along the edge of the abyss.

One other interesting fact about Millennials will bring things back to what this book is all about. Tests, show Millennials have an astronomically high expectation of the level of service they deserve. And if they don't get it, they take to their social networks and eviscerate the offending entity. They are then supported by dozens and sometimes thousands of other Tweeters and Facebookers; giving them not only instant gratification but total justification for their belief that they *deserve* the best.

Do you think this suddenly changes when they look at the company they work for and see less than perfect leadership or inadequate day-to-day management? To most, the company they work for is hopelessly out of touch and beyond repair. So they don't commit themselves emotionally. They become independent contractors who just happen to have a W-2.

What can be done?

First, you must recognize the value in being the one manager or group of executives who solves the problem. As I indicated earlier, the company that has a *sustainably* bought-in workforce can run circles around the competition, while reducing costs, turnover, and legal exposures. A company can also avoid expenditures on a number of unnecessary perks aimed at keeping employees from being totally disenfranchised, surfing the Internet while staring at the clock, or ultimately reaching for the doorknob.

It's also a humane thing. Fixing the problem will require that people no longer hate coming to work because they will no longer hate their boss. Do not blame the upcoming generation for a bad management culture. Do something about it.

As we now know from reading Chapter Three, a manager cannot establish his or her authority to lead based on personal popularity. All attempts to run for Homecoming Queen as a primary thrust will ultimately fail or leave you vulnerable when your popularity ebbs. Authority can be maintained only by one of two means, coercion or respect. Taskmasters (bosses) employ coercion. Leaders (real managers) command respect without ever overtly demanding it.

But you cannot truly lead if you are lousy at your job. If the word "manager" or the many equivalents appears in your title and you don't manage like a professional, you won't command the people's respect and you will have to resort to coercion to reinforce your authority. Since most companies no longer offer true management training, they are asking their management teams to wing it. We don't do that with almost any other profession. I'm glad my doctor and the guys flying the airplane aren't making it up as they go, based mostly on an intuitive sense of how it all works in their line of business. But somehow, it's okay if the managers who are responsible for all of your employees' production and well-being get there (or not) by successive approximations based on what did and didn't work the last time they dealt with those troublesome Earthlings.

One of the things Tom Watson, Sr. did when he founded IBM was instill a sense of pride in the company. He had in mind the culture he wanted to create for respect, decency, and a shared desire for excellence. He was also smart enough to know that he could never transmit that sense from top to bottom without having a professional management team. We had no supervisors at IBM. You were either a manager or an employee. You were not a hybrid or a fulltime HOW guy (i.e. a professional pest). All managers were professional managers and they all represented the culture, direction and purpose of the company on a daily basis.

Let's now get practical. Here are the three must-dos to start managing in the Millennial age:

First, managers must be trained. This book has been aimed at providing the information and techniques associated with professional management. It's a good start and a handy reference but they need more. They need a class that will allow them to hear, discuss, and practice what they learn. The class needs to be taught by an experienced manager. It needs to include role play for handling difficult employee situations. I teach such a class and I will be expanding the number of instructors available. But don't wait for me. Get your people trained. Damage is being done while you wait.

I recently met with a family friend who is a Millennial. I've been providing career advice for years. He has been planning to leave a high paying job (as in 500K per year) for the last 6 years because he hates his boss. Finally, the mid-sized, Seattle-based company he works for was bought out by a company back East. The first thing that company did was put every manager through orientation and a brief management training course. The difference was almost night and day when my friend's manager returned home. The offending manager is by no means perfect but the abuse and manipulation have been greatly curtailed. He must have gotten the same wakeup – more like a psychological smack on the back of the head - that I and many of my management peers got when we attended our first year of IBM management training classes.

Second, managers must be assessed. There are a number of companies, including my own, that offer what is commonly called a 360 survey in which the manager is assessed by himself, his people, and his own manager. The surveys ask a number of questions in an attempt to determine areas of strength and weakness. My survey is designed to then segregate the responses to around 60 questions into five categories which should sound familiar by now:

- Communication
- Delegation
- Recognition of performance
- General business competence
- Teambuilding and leadership.

I typically offer this survey in advance of the management class I teach. In some cases, follow-up coaching on an individual basis is recommended.

If a manager isn't assessed, then your only way of knowing how well he or she is doing is based on what he or she tells you or from what you pick up anecdotally. That in itself is unprofessional. You must know. And if you have untrained, unprofessional managers managing other untrained, unprofessional managers, how does it ever get better? At IBM, you were not only assessed on a somewhat regular basis, you were part of a company that had a management culture. Every employee knew what a professional manager was supposed to look like and what he was supposed to do. I would consider making electronic copies of this book available to all employees. Expectations are a powerful force for change.

Finally, the company itself must be assessed. And here is where I would like to spend a little time because this step is pivotal in the process of the resolving Millennial disenfranchisement. Crucial might be a better word than pivotal because like any crux point, things can go the wrong way just as easily as they can lead upward.

Each year, a company should conduct a survey in which every employee is able to participate. Most Fortune 500 companies used to do this and it was a very serious affair. In addition to gauging the general mood, you could find out specifics such as legal exposures, a sense of industry competitiveness in terms of wages and benefits, feelings about the direction of the company's products and services, and a sense of whether or not employees feel they are being managed correctly. They know.

However, most company surveys I have seen are awful. And they really haven't changed much in over 40 years. They almost encourage greater negativity. They appear to be designed more for the company analyzing the results than they are for the employees.

Don't they get it? Employee opinion surveys are supposed to at least feel like they are designed for the employees!

Instead they are designed in such a way that people are expected to set aside their emotions and be clinically dissected in order to expose belief factoids that can be easily categorized and evaluated by a computer. Who's feeling warm about that? If ever there were a generation that you don't do that to it's the Millennials. This may disappoint the survey companies and their factory-generated formats, but opinions sometimes stem from emotions that you really ought to tap into. The questions ought to indicate that you already sort of "get it" and that you would be willing to hear something that you might not like but you actually want to know. The questions need to have a dimension to them that is human. That moves the survey from black and white to color and from planar to three-dimensional. You might have some questions about the results that aren't perfectly clear but that's life. If enough questions are asked, you will have plenty to see the patterns emerge and more than enough to go back in the follow-up sessions and explore for a little more clarity.

Once you've done it this way a couple of times, then you'll be in a situation where a lot of the unnecessary emotion has dissipated. It will be an ongoing discussion rather than an exchange of salvoes.

Let me give you an example of the subtle difference between standard survey questions, which I pulled right off the internet, and the type I would encourage my clients to use with a survey they get from me. Keep in mind, the people taking this survey will respond on a scale from *Strongly Agree* to *Strongly Disagree*.

Standard Survey: Managers in this organization are competent.

Charles' Survey: Management in this company is made up of professionals with actual management skills.

Standard Survey: Customer needs are the top priority in this organization.[15]

Charles Survey: Knowing what I know from the inside, I would be delighted to be a customer of our company.

Standard Survey: The company vision has been well articulated.

Charles' Survey: It's pretty clear to me what this company is trying to become in the next several years.

Standard Survey: This organization has good hiring standards.

Charles' Survey: There might be one or two people who aren't setting the world on fire, but for the most part we have good quality people in our company.

The survey companies are collecting data. I'm trying to start a dialogue with employees to find things out and then begin the process of working things out. The survey company employs statisticians and industrial psychologists. I have actually run a company and have had to live with the results of surveys. Which of us do you identify with?

When a client sees my kind of survey, they will want to tweak the wording just a bit. This creates a lot more work for me but that's exactly what you should do. You see the potential nuances and the power therein. It suddenly makes the standard survey questions look not only vapid and impersonal but lame in terms of telling you much. For example, do you want to hope that people know the purpose of a vision statement or do you want to see if yours is actually understood

---

[15] The *top priority?* Is this really the time to remind them that the customer is viewed by the company as a higher priority than the person taking the survey? Go back and read pages 166 to 168 to learn how this can suck the life out of a company. The employee is the top priority of companies who employ Earthlings. What other old fashioned thoughts will you and this survey company placard?

and working? Do you want to have people guess what your hiring standards are or do you want to know if they think you're doing a good job of bringing in and developing good talent?

Other management consulting companies have their proprietary surveys and I have my survey approach. Regardless of which you use, it should have the following characteristics:

- It must be anonymous, yet be traceable by employee group to *individual* managers.

- It must allow for write-in comments. It must encourage them.

- It needs to have elements that can be replicated and tracked on a year-to-year basis. IBM had a built-in Morale Index which was based on answers to five specific questions dispersed throughout the survey. Interestingly, one of these five was the degree of trust and confidence each employee had in his or her direct report manager. If you as a manager had less than 59% positive in this category, you ran a risk of not keeping your job. You would certainly be questioned.

- It should include questions about major undertakings or events in the last year. It is not only important to know how new plans and programs are working, it is important to avoid looking like a canned survey. People want relevance, not recycling. Besides, you might learn something.

- Turnaround on posting the results should be expeditious.

Communication of the results should be handled with incredible comprehensiveness and responsiveness. The CEO should give a summary and talk about how important the survey is. He or she must make it clear that changes will be made and the implementation of company plans will be modified based on what came out of the survey. It can't be an appeasement or a mea culpa. It needs to come across as a group of professional executives giving a sober response to input from a group of professional employees.

Individual managers or at least 2nd-level managers should get their people together and not only discuss the results, but seek further input. Again, it can't be an apology. It must be taken as it is intended. It is a part of a process of determining how the company will operate. Even if it results in major actions, those actions must be clearly seen to be at the discretion and instigation of the leadership team. Nobody wants to believe that they are working for a company that is run by the consent of the masses and the last poll. Read the discussion on consensus management (page 56). It weakens companies.

Finally, don't be surprised by the apparent vitriol and downright animosity that you receive in the results of the first survey or if it has been a while. This is quite common, especially if employees view this as their one shot to express those feelings they have been harboring for a long time. When I took over a company that had 700 miserable employees and I started going to some of the larger job sites, I got an earful. Microsoft was one of our largest clients. We had over 100 software developers out there. In my first ever employee forum held on site at the Microsoft facility, I saw faces with lips curled, eyes narrowed, noses wrinkled in anger and disdain for me and the company I was now leading. But by about the third meeting, it was more like, "Hey, Charles, I've got an idea for how we could handle this or that item a little better."

It is critical that people know that communication is going to be ongoing. This is not their last chance to be heard *and responded* to.

What did I do in those first couple of meetings besides listen? First, I responded to their input. But I didn't do it in a patronizing fashion. In some cases, after a particularly nasty outburst, I would ask if it was really that dark or was there a better way of breaking down the problem and giving me something I could actually respond to. In some cases, I would say, "Think about that for a moment and I'll come back to you." Or "I want to hear more about that. Let's talk for a bit after the meeting."[16]

When it came to suggestions, I was real clear about what I felt I could do something about and what I was probably not going to deal with. I would often say, "With all that's on our plate, that's just not something I feel the company can take on at this stage." I never responded hostilely nor did I try to make someone feel stupid for what should have been seen as a dumb idea. Do that and the flow of new thoughts will dry up. Diplomacy is not an option. It is a part of management.

In terms of responding, as a CEO I had to avoid becoming the surrogate first-line manager for everyone. A well-coordinated response through the management hierarchy was critical. Employees must believe in the efficacy of the office of the person they report to. If you become the master to-do guy, you will have neutered your entire management team. Doing so is the CEO version of running for Homecoming Queen. You can't win because everyone knows it's unsustainable.

My thoughts on the Millennial problem cannot in all practicality go too much deeper than what I have just described. But in concluding, I would like to address something I mentioned earlier - companies allowing a portion of their employee population to work from home. I can only do so briefly without knowing more about a company; but inherently, I don't like the idea. It makes sense in some cases but it also depends on what problem you're trying to solve. It should be aimed at

---

[16] Can you pronounce sangfroid? Here's your chance to use it. By the way, I like mine shaken, not stirred.

solving individual problems on an employee by employee basis. It should not be a case of giving up on having any kind of culture or atmosphere. When the new CEO for Yahoo! issued her controversial edict that people needed to come back to the office to work, she wasn't promoting efficiency. Studies show that on an individual basis, productivity is about the same for at-home versus office dwelling employees. But what she was thinking about was teambuilding, culture, rapid communication, and effective companywide problem solving.

Of course you need to work with single parents or special situations. In those cases technology is a blessing. But ultimately, you've got to decide what your company is going to be like and then you need to have a sense of what that would "feel" like. Only then can you answer the question about having lots of independent, physically disconnected employees. But when you think about it, how far off from disenfranchised is disconnected? And isn't that the problem regarding Millennials that we were trying to address in the first place? Operating from home a day or two a week probably isn't going to sabotage camaraderie and buy-in. But anything more than that and you have something other than that sense of tribe that is built into every one of us. The question is, whose tribe will they belong to if they don't feel part of yours?

Summary of Concepts
A Lefthander's Guide to Management

To some people, left-handed thinking is simply untoward or not quite right. To others, especially those with a lefty in the family, you realize that we simply look at life just a little bit differently. Lefties can be handy to have around, especially if you are stuck on a problem that just won't seem to present a clear opening for resolution. Then sometimes, we simply can't look at a problem the same way as everyone else, which makes it really handy to have right-handed people around.

Using a different lens and operating as a pre-med student who was always planning to leave the business world and go back to medicine, I built a way of looking at management that was useful to me. It made sense. It simplified things and then it let me use these simplified concepts to build new approaches to leading people and running a company. And then I wrote a book about it.

These are the concepts I present when I speak to groups of executives about management in general. They are also the concepts I adapt when I am asked to address hot topics such as the emergence of the Millennial culture and what to do about it. I suppose I look at this latter topic a bit differently as well. I think it's a great opportunity – if you don't drop the ball on the fundamentals of good management and decent behavior.

Most of these concepts were covered at various places in the book. Some are from other books I have written or they came from speaking engagements. Many of these are fairly unique, I am told.

But some of them have been brought forth by others and I choose to put a different spin on them or merely reemphasize them because I think they have prematurely and inappropriately fallen into desuetude.

They're grouped logically to some extent and randomly here and there. That's the left-handed way.

A Manager Defined

1. Focus on What, not How. This has been the theme of this book.
2. Your job is to create problems for your people to solve. You are not the hero problem solver for your department. Identify the problems, set the objectives, measure the results, provide feedback and guidance. Repeat.
3. Management is a profession, not merely a role in a company.
4. Never forget the super-simplified role of a manager is to have the right people doing the right things. Get too far beyond that and you're a supervisor. That's a glorified word for a boss. Everyone wants a great manager and a true leader. Nobody wants a boss.
5. Deal in business issues, not personalities. You're a professional manager not a psychologist. You're a leader, not a manipulator.
6. A manager is a coach and counselor not a judge; a manager is a leader not a referee.
7. You are a manager because you have management skills. This is how it should be. It's not because you're smart or

you sold the most widgets. EQ is way more important than IQ. I've got a lot of bruises from when I thought otherwise.

8. The most important desire a leader must have to be successful is to serve. Does that sound sanctimonious? Kind of a throwaway line that nobody dares argue with but you're all thinking, "That's a bunch of …stuff." But if a key business goal is to take care of the client and the employees are your front line for doing that, shouldn't you be doing everything to make sure they are able to do so? Figure out what they need to get their job done and then give it to them. That's service.

Vision and Purpose of your company

9. A great vision statement does not merely tell you what you are aiming to accomplish in the future; it changes who you are right now. I was just a kid but I remember Kennedy saying that by the end of the decade we were going to put a man on the moon. That got us out of the tit-for-tat race with the Soviet Union where they launched a satellite and then we launched a satellite; they sent a man into space and we sent a man into space. It changed who we were. Instantly, we were no longer the "me too" guys, we were the guys who were going to the moon!

10. If you know who you are, you will know what to do. This is true for people as well as companies and organizations.

11. Average people believe you have to do a lot of things or do something big to be successful. Great people realize you have to be someone.

12. A true vision statement is complete and includes the mission and major milestones that when achieved will make the vision possible. If you present a vision statement without indicating you know and have a plan for the obvious big hurdles you will encounter, people won't buy in. Go read Kennedy's speech on going to the moon. He talks about all the things we would need to do to make it happen, including us believing we could do it.

13. Know what business you are really in. It's almost never in the name of your company. It tells you what your most important function is. When Xerox realized they were in the document management business and Harley realized they were in the nostalgia business, their fortunes turned around. Blue Cross is in the claims processing business. Starbucks is not in the coffee business. What business are you in?

14. Use the two hoops theory for every department. If you fire a missile at two imaginary hoops in the sky, separated by several miles, and it makes it through both hoops, you are likely to hit your target. Know the two key measurements for each department and then don't bug 'em about the other ones unless they miss one of the hoops.

15. Avoid parallax – thinking you're all lined up on the same corporate objective when you really aren't. If a manager only a couple of levels down from the CEO makes his targets, the CEO should make his. But the CEO has to know for sure. Know your top two objectives and then find out what the top two objectives of your direct reports are plus

the top two objectives of his direct reports are. It takes 10 minutes. By the way, your direct reports should know two levels down as well.

16. I never wanted to know more than the one or two key things any of my direct reports were pursuing. Anything beyond that I could call his or her secretary and ask. Work on big stuff. And make sure your direct reports are working on big stuff.

Manager as a coach and counselor

17. You must earn the right to criticize, even if you're the boss. To truly criticize you must already be established as a trusted collaborator, well in advance. This is critical when dealing with Millennials.

18. Performance must become a third party object that you and the employee can put on the table and discuss. Do this even if the employee is way behind: "Fred, you were supposed to be at point X but you're only at point Y, what's needed to close the gap? What can I do to help?"

19. If you have made it clear to the employee that you are there to help them in their career and working only in their best interest, then and only then, can you treat performance like a third party object.

20. Never ask adults to justify themselves or their behavior. Avoid the use of the word "Why?" When you ask, "What happened?" it makes people a lot less defensive than when you say, "Why did you do that?" By the way, the age at which this gives better results starts at 4 years old. Try it.

21. Certain management types will never be in position to offer ongoing coaching and counseling. If your style requires that people defend themselves even occasionally, they will do that first and then maybe they'll talk about business objectively – but probably not. Survival trumps business.

22. Powder puff appraisals, focusing only on the positive, are a copout and an extension of the self-esteem movement. It's essentially an admission of failure to establish trust.

23. When critiquing or giving feedback, talk about general reaction and overall positives first. Talk about the big stuff and then the little stuff. Discuss negatives only if you have to and then secondarily. Consider mentioning trivial stuff in a separate, oh-by-the-way conversation to avoid looking trivial or making the employee feel like something trivial just took away from his or her good work. Think about how you feel when you are criticized. I personally hate it. This is mostly due to a lifetime of being counseled by insensitive jerks, who have taken advantage of their position to treat a subordinate in a way they would never treat someone whose relationship they truly valued.

Decision Making

24. Decisions are made by verifying a gut feel, not by weighing the pros and cons. You're an executive, not an accountant. You will always have less information than you need for big decisions.

25. Make the decision and then clean up the mess.

26. Big decisions almost always hurt someone. Big decisions that are delayed hurt almost everyone.

27. Seeking consensus is for weaklings. Allow for constant input. Collaborate to the extent necessary and then make the decision.

Humane Management and Tribal Instincts

28. Humane management has two components: Caring and Competence. Caring alone won't do it. Working for a manager who is lousy at the many functions of management is miserable. It hurts people who count on you. It's inhumane.

29. Caring is an act not a feeling. Compassion is a feeling. True caring is putting compassion into action.

30. We are tribal creatures with an innate desire to belong permanently. Make people feel secure, even if it costs you in a specific instance.

31. The industrial revolution was the first time we made an institution out of non-tribal behaviors in that for the first time people could routinely be kicked out of the tribe at will. By continuing this practice, we are creating an environment that defies 2 million years of human development.

32. Note to CEOs: You are the head of your tribe. Your number one constituency is your people, not your customers, not your shareholders. Never forget that. And never let your people forget that you won't forget that. CEOs who say the customer is number one are abrading delicate human instincts and making it clear that their people are just cogs

in an organic machine. Making sure your customers and shareholders think they are at the top of your list falls under the CEO function called diplomacy.

Morale and the three Utility functions of management

33. You can manage morale via two levers: Creating a sense that the company is going to do well and regularly performing the utility functions of management:
    a. Communication
    b. Delegation
    c. Recognition of performance

34. People must feel heard. It's not good enough that you hear them. They must feel it. If they don't they'll find someone else who will make them feel heard. That other person may not be acting in your best interest or the company's best interest. That's the practical reason. The humane reason is that it hurts not to be heard. People today often feel very lonely at work. Fix that.

35. Good and timely communication makes people feel valued, not just informed.

36. Employee opinion surveys are too often viewed by the employee as their one shot at letting you know how messed up things are. It should not be that way. The opinion survey is a process that should have employee involvement even in the design. Employees need to know it will be an iterative process with multiple avenues for feedback. If companies fail to do this, they will simply be setting themselves up for

the biggest salvos the employees can launch to make sure they get heard and maybe even responded to.

37. Delegation makes people feel good about themselves. It gives them worth. Done right, it allows people to achieve *your* objectives *their* way, which is always more efficient and effective. It allows them to think about it long enough to perhaps come back and tell you that they ought not to do it at all. Only great managers have this kind of relationship with their direct reports.

38. Some people can't delegate even if they want to. If you are a perfectionist or in any way punitive, people won't do it their way, they will spend all their time trying to figure out how you would like them to do it. Start cutting your people some slack for your own good. That may sound selfish but if you're perfectionist or punitive, you're already a selfish person. I'm just giving you some tips and appealing to the only avenue open to persuade you.

39. Recognition is done in a variety of ways, every day. If people aren't recognized for their work, they feel devalued. Who wants a bunch of people working for them who feel lousy about themselves? I'll tell you, egotists who have a need to be the most important and valuable person. If you can't get there on merit, then devalue others. Productivity suffers but egotists feel bigger somehow.

40. People who constantly make people feel like they should have done a little better are true jerks. Some people think this is a clever way to get people to close the performance gap. It's not. It makes people give up and then adopt a

variety of masking behaviors to get by. Millennials won't even fake it. They're too honest. They'll just shut down.

41. Most managers can't list three reasons why their employees come to work every day. That's sad. What's even sadder is that most employees can't either. Give them lots of reasons.

Management Power

42. Great managers increase their power by extending maximum power to the people that report to them. It almost defies the laws of physics. I'm as fascinated by this as I am by hydraulics and compound interest. It's magic. Try it.

43. Power comes from two sources: Respect or some form of coercion. Leaders are respected and can draw on the power in people to get things done. Bosses must use energy to get people moving and keep them moving.

44. If you aren't any good at the job of managing, people will eventually have little respect for you and you will have to resort to coercion in its many forms. Managers need training.

45. Moody managers divert people's energy. Your employees go from solving business problems to appeasing your moods and timing their actions or requests for your "good" days. How is that good for business?

46. Another form of coercion is trying to be popular. As a manager, never run for Homecoming Queen. You'll lose, even if you're the only one running. You can't lead based on popularity and people liking you. It's a pitiful form of coercion.

Turnover

47. Turnover is a consequence of disconnectedness. You must have a strategy that makes people feel both secure and connected. Some people call this disenfranchisement. I would use that word if I thought anyone I asked could define "enfranchisement."

48. Turnover prevention begins at hiring. Employee orientation as a goal in itself is inadequate. The goal must be assimilation and there must be a formal program, involving multiple levels of managers over an extended period of time.

49. People quit most often because of a fear of their own imminent failure in their performance or in their relationships. Institute programs that make it nearly impossible to fire employees and people will no longer quit. Instead, they will divert their energies from defense to offense and start trying to get ahead.

50. Never let a person feel they have permanently fallen from grace.

51. Firing someone is a violent act. You harm or destroy families, career plans, college plans, retirement plans. You are firing a spouse and kids too.

52. When you fire someone it has a systemic effect. It disrupts people's sense of security throughout the company. Firing someone who deserves it is not okay either. One thing people should never pray for is justice. I thank God, literally, that I haven't always gotten what I deserve. You

should too. Now pay that forward and show the lack of justice you've benefited from for decades.

53. Not firing someone who deserves it demonstrates grace and mercy and improves people's sense of security. In a company of 100 or more employees, you can almost always find another role for the person. You have many levers to pull besides firing: reassignment, demotion, pay cuts until they are back on track, etc. Be creative. There's a real human being and his or her family involved.

Solving the supposed Millennial "Crisis"

54. View it as an incredible opportunity. If you can't do that, please tell me how you're going to skip an entire generation. There are 82 million of them. I work with them all the time. They are sharp. Sometimes they seem rude but they're so honest and coachable, you can just point out stuff that bugs you – unless of course you have zero relationship with them. If that's the case get used to people texting while you're telling them about your mother's last words on her deathbed.

55. Millennials are incredibly underutilized. Millennials got well educated, were told they could be anything they set their mind on becoming, and then when they hatched in about 2006, the world fell apart. They got screwed. They are chronically depressed. Start treating them well and see what happens. Start giving them real assignments and big jobs. You'll be amazed. They're just like us.

56. Follow the three "secret" investment strategies I learned while I was at IBM:

    a. Invest during downturns while everyone else is hiding under their desk.

    b. Invest in management. It's an asset layer, not overhead. Get some ROI out of it. People quit investing in management training about a decade ago and look where we are now with awful morale and high turnover.

    c. Only hire A players. They are worth three times as much as B players but they don't cost three times as much.

57. You must do three counter-intuitive things with Millennials

    a. Depersonalize the management process to improve your personal relationship with all employees. That's what this whole book has been about. If you can't get performance to the level of an object discussed by two colleagues, you are not going to cut it with Millennials or anyone else. They'll quit and move back home. Over one third of them have done it.

    b. You must commit to the relationship first. Giving them a job is not a personal commitment. Did you use up a hiring ticket? Big deal. They just changed their life to come work for you. The days of giving up one's whole life for the company are over. So get out in front of it.

    c. To the extent possible, adjust to their lifestyle. It's not that hard. It's the way work has been done for all but about two hundred of the last two million years. I'm a laissez faire capitalist but I honestly can't distinguish much between old style industrialism and slavery. The world is going to change. The question we have as managers and executives is this: are we going to lead that change or are we going to have it happen to us?

Two things I frequently say to clients who are in difficulty:

58. You don't have 17 problems, you have one or two. Let's figure them out and the other 15 or 16 will recede in importance or, better said, urgency.

59. You are not going to fine-tune your way out of this mess. You need to take bold action and you have to be right. Just because you're surrounded, doesn't mean you can attack in any direction. Let's find the right place to focus your energy and then apply everything you've got.

Universal rule for what to do.

60. We all play multiple roles in life: Father, mother, son, brother, daughter, sister, neighbor, coach, teacher, manager, employer, peer, coworker, ex-husband, citizen. The list goes on and changes from time to time. What doesn't change is the need to play these roles unilaterally. In other words, be the best at what you do, regardless of how the other person in the relationship plays their role. Never make it contingent. Don't be the best brother only if your sister is the best sister. If you screwed up as a husband and the marriage fell apart, understand what she's going through

now with the kids and be a great ex. Don't be the best coach only if the athlete does everything he or she should. Take action and use discipline but don't withhold doing a great job. When that athlete, student, or employee leaves your charge someday, make sure he or she says, "He was the best coach, teacher, manager, I ever had."

ABOUT THE AUTHOR

Charles is a Seattle native and a longtime resident of planet Earth. He married Kristy while in college and he feels that was the best decision of his life. They have three great kids, Lexie, Mason and Walker, along with llamas, two chickens and a bulldog named Bullard, who is very dull and dependent.

With a Bachelor of Science degree in pre-medical studies and fresh out of the University of Washington, Charles took the next logical step. He started his career at IBM in the group that sold the behemoth mainframes, despite the fact that he was the only one of 228 applicants that had never seen a computer.

He diligently stuck with his preparations to go to medical school for over 17 years, moving in and out of IBM field and headquarters jobs. Finally, it was time. He left his position as the head of the IBM consulting group in the Northwest and took over as CEO for a high-end micro-roaster in the burgeoning Seattle coffee market.

With a solid understanding of both regular and decaf, he then stepped in and ran a large software integration firm, building it from 700 (mostly miserable) employees to where it was the dominant IT consulting firm in the Northwest, with over 1500 (mostly happy) employees. Next, he and his colleague Bill Douglass started and sold their own IT consulting firm.

Of the 5000 people in Seattle who have worked for Charles at one time or another, approximately 80% love him; 15% could take him or leave him; and 5% will run him over in a crosswalk if they see him. This is an admirable distribution and one we should all strive for – especially if you look both ways when crossing the street.

He took a multi-year sabbatical and went alone to the mud huts of Kenya, the slums of Bombay, Afghanistan and other places rarely mentioned in Condé Nast. There he resolved an epidemic, treated lepers and untouchables for all kinds of health ailments, and taught a woman to walk again who had been crippled for 33 years. He is now reluctantly back in the business world where he would prefer to consult rather than work.

Charles also competes internationally in Masters Track and Field in the 400 meter dash. In 2012 he was the Silver Medalist in the 400 meters at the USA Track and Field Masters National Championships in Chicago.

Charles is the author of *Breath of Kenya*, which details his time in a primitive village in the deep interior of East Africa.

Check out his other books listed at the beginning

Email the author: charles@charlesherrick.com

www.ingramcontent.com/pod-product-compliance
Lightning Source LLC
Chambersburg PA
CBHW031826170526
45157CB00001B/195